WATERSI
In Linc

Brett Collier

COUNTRYSIDE BOOKS
NEWBURY, BERKSHIRE

First published 1999
© Brett Collier 1999

COUNTRYSIDE BOOKS
3 Catherine Road
Newbury, Berkshire

ISBN 1 85306 571 4

Designed by Graham Whiteman
Cover illustration by Colin Doggett
Maps and photographs by the author

Produced through MRM Associates Ltd., Reading
Printed by J. W. Arrowsmith Ltd., Bristol

Contents

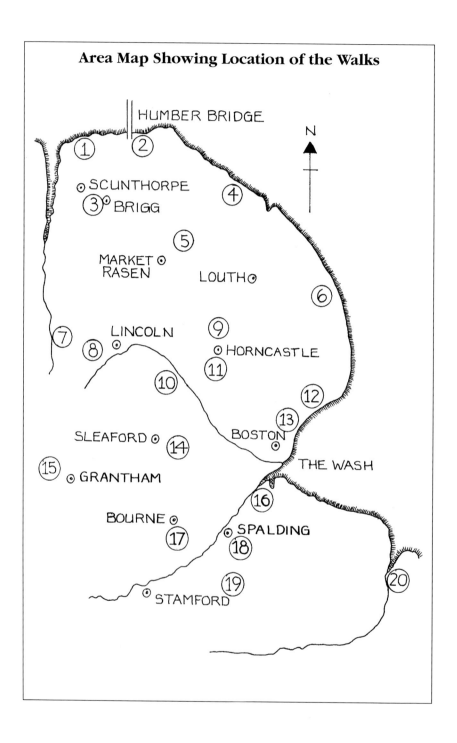

Area Map Showing Location of the Walks

Walk

To Janet, who held the fort yet again.

Publisher's Note

We hope that you obtain considerable enjoyment from this book; great care has been taken in its preparation. Although at the time of publication all routes followed public rights of way or permitted paths, diversion orders can be made and permissions withdrawn.

We cannot of course be held responsible for such diversion orders and any inaccuracies in the text which result from these or any other changes to the routes nor any damage which might result from walkers trespassing on private property. We are anxious though that all details covering the walks are kept up to date and would therefore welcome information from readers which would be relevant to future editions.

INTRODUCTION

In Lincolnshire you can be spoilt for choice when it comes to choosing a waterside walk. To the Romans the River Trent was not an obstacle but a resource and they increased its usefulness by linking the Rivers Trent and Witham with a man-made canal, the Fossdyke, which connects Lincoln with Torksey and is said to be the oldest navigable canal in use in the country. One of the walks in North Lincolnshire visits Wintringham Haven where the Romans used a Humber crossing for their journey northwards to York, another uses the lovely little one-arched bridge over the infant River Welland at West Deeping on the King Street Roman road. The Lincolnshire coast had mile after mile of Roman sea defences although today many of them are far inland. Roman banks are met at Wrangle and on the other side of the county, a walk takes you by the site of a fort at the end of a long, straight Roman road commanding a historic river crossing of the Trent to a hamlet once named Segelocum. At each of these places and many others throughout the county there is strong evidence, even today, of Roman civil engineering skills. Yet there is much more to be found on these walks. You will encounter smugglers on Lincolnshire's lonely coastline and Cromwell and King Harold marching to battle. All around are the visible signs of man's centuries-old fight with the encroaching sea, whether you are walking along a sea bank or by one of the Drains that cross the flat land. There are historic canals, as at Tetney Lock, and fascinating old towns, such as Spalding on the River Welland or Lincoln and the Fossdyke. Our present day concern with conservation is apparent in places as diverse as the old clay pits at Barton on Humber that are now a series of lakes rich in plants and wildlife, or along the Peter Scott Way on the very rim of the Wash.

Each walk either starts from or near a pub, or passes a named pub en route. Do remember though that details given about inns are subject to change and therefore telephone numbers have been given for you to confirm whatever arrangement you wish to make. In most cases landlords have readily agreed that cars may be left while you are doing a walk but unfortunately today a strange car on the car park out of normal opening hours may sometimes be regarded as suspicious. Leaving a note that you are doing the walk and expect to be back for at least a drink is a friendly gesture that will be welcomed upon your return.

Sketch maps are provided to offer details of the particular walk with identifying numbered paragraphs along the route but the ability to use and read an Ordnance Survey map to check various features will greatly enhance one's enjoyment of the countryside and the relevant OS Landranger map is noted for each walk.

Suggestions are also given for places of interest, should you wish to lengthen your day out in the area.

Please respect the life of the countryside and try to obey the Country Code whenever it is possible to do so, particularly by removing litter. It is important though to attempt to keep to the correct line of any public right of way and remember that it is not you who are committing an offence by doing so. Detouring around a field edge to avoid crops only leads to confusion for other walkers and may leave you open to a charge that you were nowhere near a public right of way. Most walkers are welcome in the countryside and villagers have often remarked that it is good to see people walking their paths. Farmers do worry about dogs harming their livestock though so please keep dogs under close control.

No crowded or feet-eroded fieldpaths here – for one of the attractions of walking in Lincolnshire is that it is still possible to walk on public paths away from roads and to meet hardly anyone en route, except perhaps in the villages. Do enjoy your Waterside Walks as much as I have in selecting them.

Brett Collier

Acknowledgement

With thanks to *Lincolnshire Life* magazine for authority to publish information from an article on ley lines.

BY PUDDING PIE SANDS

A marvellous walk with views across the Humber in this strangely remote north-west corner of Lincolnshire. Field paths lead from Winteringham to Whitton, and then the walk is along river embankments to arrive at the tiny Winteringham Haven, full of interest with its diverse array of sea-going boats.

Winteringham Haven.

Throughout history the rivers Trent and Humber, which meet a few miles to the west, were the main route between the Midlands and the German Ocean. The mouth of the Humber was also the obvious invasion route for the wild Norsemen who came initially for plunder and eventually settled in the area. The Romans had also found the estuary strategically important. The limestone ridge that runs all the way from Stamford in the south of the county finally disappears into the Humber hereabouts and the Roman Ermine Street followed closely parallel on the east of this ridge from Stamford to Ancaster, through Lincoln, to reach the Humber at Flashmere Haven, near Winteringham and opposite the eastern end of Pudding Pie Sands. From Flashmere Haven Roman soldiers were ferried across the river to Brough, and so on to York, and around the haven the Roman town of Ad Abum is believed to have been built. Half a century ago Lord Noel Buxton set out to test the theory that the Humber used to be forded by the Romans near here. He waded across the river from Whitton and was only thwarted by deeper water near the Yorkshire shore. However, in ancient times, before the shores were embanked, the waters of the Humber would have spread more widely into the Winteringham Ings of the Ancholme valley and the low-lying Yorkshire shores, so it was then more shallow and so fordable at low tide. This is not a waterway to be treated lightly today. Whitton Ness, a little to the east of the village, pokes out into mid-channel and this combined with Whitton Sand in mid-stream and the current and tides of the Humber, along Whitton Channel past Devil's Causeway, makes navigation a tricky business.

At one time, when the ferry across the Humber ran from here, there were five pubs in Winteringham plus the famous Tinkle Brewery renowned for its ales and stouts. However, silting of the river became so bad that by 1810 the ferry had to be moved to South Ferriby Sluice. Today, only two pubs remain, the Ferry Boat and the Bay Horse. The Bay Horse is a welcome and popular Free House with a fine selection of real ales and lagers, including Lambton's Smooth Blended Beer, Ward's Best Bitter, Vaux's Double Maxim Premium Ale, Samson Cask Ale, Vaux Mild and Heineken Cold Filtered Lager Beer. There are hot and cold bar snacks and traditional and special home-made food including their particular specialities of Fondue Bourguignonne and Chocolate Fondue that obviously need to be ordered in advance. Meals are served from 12 noon until 2 pm and from 7 pm until 9 pm each day, including Sunday. The inn is open for drinking from 12 noon until 11 pm every day except Sunday when it closes at 10.30 pm. Three en suite rooms are available although I'm told there is a mischievous ghost. Dick Turpin is reputed to have stayed here.

Telephone: 01724 732865.

- **HOW TO GET THERE:** Follow Ermine Street Roman road (B1207) for 9½ miles northwards from the A18(T) and the M180 junction roundabout, signposted Broughton and Winterton. Cross northwards over the A1077. From Scunthorpe turn left off the Barton upon Humber A1077 road to Winteringham at a sharp right-hand bend, 9 miles north of Scunthorpe.

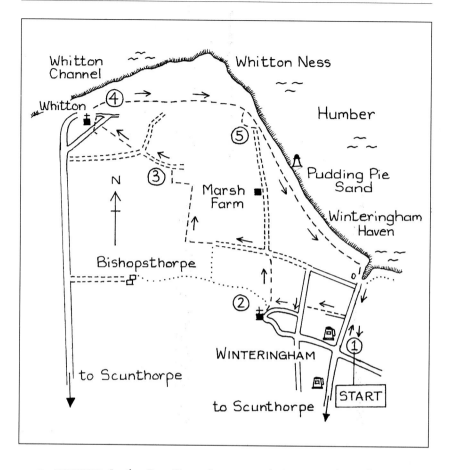

- **PARKING:** In the Bay Horse Inn car park, Winteringham (by kind permission of the landlady).
- **LENGTH OF THE WALK:** 6 easy miles. Map: OS Landranger 112 Scunthorpe and surrounding area (GR 931222).

THE WALK

1 From the inn car park turn left down Low Burbage for 300 yards and then left again up the signposted path with an unusual long, high wall on your immediate left. At the kissing gate go straight forward on FP 316 to Marsh Lane. The signposts in North Lincolnshire very helpfully include the fieldpath numbers. On reaching the lane turn left and then right at Western Green to Meggitt Lane and All Saints church and churchyard.

2 At the beginning of the church wall in Meggitt Lane follow the signposted track (FP 14). Where the farm track turns left after a few yards proceed straight forward to a good footbridge with handrails over the Haven Drain and a three-fingered signpost. Ignore the path on the left indicated to Bishopsthorpe and follow the well defined footpath to Waterside. On reaching the lane leading down to Marsh Farm turn left along the signposted wide farm track for 800 yards. Fifty yards from the Rotten Sykes public footpath coming from the left, turn right on a diverted, signposted path keeping the dyke on your immediate right. Turn left at the field end to a footbridge.

3 Cross the footbridge and continue straight forward towards the farm with a deep dyke on your left. Turn left on reaching the good track just before the farm. About 200 yards beyond the track junction leave the track to proceed diagonally left across the field, aiming for the left hand edge of the hedge across the field to your front. Upon reaching the hedge (waymark) continue forward on the same line and cross an earth bridge to a green lane with some development over on the left. Turn left along this green lane. Where the lane turns to the left leave the track to turn right towards Whitton church by a concrete gatepost (no gate) with a waymark. Walk on to Post Office Lane and turn right with Amen Cottage on the right. At the road bend with Chapel Lane go straight forward on the public footpath with the church and graveyard on your immediate left.

4 Turn right on reaching the road at the foot of Church Hill and continue for 200 yards until the road ends. Turn left on a signposted footpath, initially along the embanked line of the old railway with a three-fingered signpost with one arm indicating Winteringham. Follow the top of the embankment (or below it if the wind is too keen) on the clear path past Whitton Ness.

5 Come to the path junction and motorable track leading down to Marsh Farm – with the intriguing name of Booth Nookin Lane (FP 314) and the stern signpost warning: 'Leave your gun at home. Armed trespassers on the marsh will be prosecuted'! Continue along the top of the embankment for 1¼ miles past Pudding Pie Sand to Winteringham Haven. Passing the club house of the Yacht Club on the right, turn right down to the lane. At the lane turn left over the road bridge and continue straight up the lane for 700 yards to the Bay Horse Inn.

One of the two pubs in the village.

PLACES OF INTEREST NEARBY

Five miles down the road from Winteringham, via West Halton, is the interesting village of *Alkborough* that is well worth a visit. This is part of a scenic drive for there are extensive views from the Cliff ridge overlooking Trent Falls where the rivers Trent and Ouse become the Humber. Indeed, under the right conditions it is said that you can see York Minster. En route the Humber Bridge may also be seen. The grass maze at Julian's Bower, Alkborough is believed to have been made by monks in the 12th century and in the fine oak porch of the church there is a stone replica of the maze.

AROUND BARTON UPON HUMBER

An easy but fascinating walk over level ground around the ancient town of Barton upon Humber. Here you can enjoy the wonder and beauty of the modern bridge, a country park, Far Ings Nature Reserve and a splendid watering hole towards the end of the walk. All against the backdrop of the wide sweep of the Humber.

The Humber Bridge.

Barton upon Humber, by the late 10th century, was the most important town in North Lincolnshire, having a ferry across the Humber, two water mills and one of the county's seven recorded markets. Its trading activities throughout the Middle Ages included the import and export of products such as wine, fish, hides, wool and foodstuffs. By 1900 brick and tile making, boat building, rope making, agricultural, chemical and bicycle manufacture were some of the industries established in Barton. The series of lakes beside the Humber embankment are old flooded clay workings that are being developed into a linear Country Park that stretches over 5 miles. The task of the

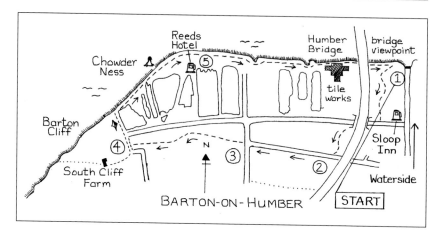

Project Officer was to achieve a balance between recreational needs such as yachting, wind surfing, fishing and canoeing and the wildlife conservation of this unique area. Along this low-lying plain next to the Humber the extensive man-made workings form the largest area of freshwater marsh in the region. Their varying depths have created a mixture of dense reed beds and open waters bordered by scrub woodland and grassland, all of which supports a variety of wildlife. Because of their conservation importance the majority of pits are scheduled as Sites of Special Scientific Interest. The Far Ings Reserve has five viewing hides, shallow and deep water areas, reed beds, woodland and well maintained pathways. Visitors are welcome but are asked to keep to the paths and not to allow dogs onto the reserve.

Reeds Hotel, on the return section of the walk, is well worth a call for rather superior refreshment. Bar meals are served in the Four Seasons Lounge Bar with its beamed ceiling and inglenook fireplace. There is a patio overlooking one of the two lakes. Ward's Bitter, Stella Artois lager, draught Guinness and Strongbow cider are available, as well as freshly brewed coffee or a choice of teas (Earl Grey, Yorkshire, Ceylon or Darjeeling) and hot chocolate. Cream teas, a selection of sandwiches with brown or white bread and a children's menu may also be obtained. Unusually, it is a No Smoking hotel.
Telephone: 01652 632313.

* **HOW TO GET THERE:** Coming from the north across the bridge simply turn left into Barton upon Humber. Coming from Brigg or Scunthorpe you will find all roads lead to the bridge but take care to turn off into

Barton upon Humber itself before you are committed into crossing the bridge. The Humber Bridge Viewing Point and Country Park, starting point for this walk, is signposted through the town.

- **PARKING:** In the car park at the Humber Bridge Viewing Point and Country Park.
- **LENGTH OF THE WALK:** 3½ miles. Map: OS Landranger 112 Scunthorpe and surrounding area (GR 028234).

THE WALK

1 From the car park climb the embankment and turn left towards the bridge, perhaps after visiting the Tourist Information Centre building just on the right (and the start of the Viking Way, Lincolnshire's first long distance recreational path, a 138 mile recreational walk beginning at Barton and ending at Oakham in Rutland). Walking towards the bridge disregard the first lot of steps leading back into the car park but take the second steps some 50 yards further on. Turn right with the pond on the right. Cross two footbridges between ponds and then walk down the wide grass track to the road. Turn right on reaching Far Ings Road to walk forward under the road that leads to the bridge embankment.

2 Immediately beyond the road bridge turn left off Far Ings Road to follow the signposted, permissive path on the right. It is marked 'Dam Road ½ km'. Continue on the clear but winding track through the trees until you reach Dam Road. Turn right along the road for 900 yards until you reach the T-junction.

3 Walk straight ahead at the end of the road to follow the stiled, bridged and signposted public footpath marked 'South Ferriby 3½ km'. Follow this meandering path with the hedge on the left.

4 At the end of this footpath cross the ditch by the footbridge with a hedge on your immediate left. Turn right on a good, motorable track signposted 'Byway'. On reaching the Humber embankment turn right through the metal kissing gate with the lake on the right. Pass Chowder Ness navigation indicator and some 500 yards further on turn right, if you so wish, down the embankment steps to Reeds Hotel.

Reed mace, water forget-me-not, brooklime, water plantain and fool's watercress may be seen, with celery-leafed buttercup and wild celery, at Far Ings Nature Reserve. Quite a lot of alders have been planted for they are not found as a wild tree in this area. Major features of the Clay Pits are the magnificent old hawthorn hedges that thrive on the heavy clay. In the past five years the Clay Pits have gained a few new breeding species of birds such as the greylag goose, ruddy duck and possibly the sparrowhawk. Collared doves, lesser whitethroats and Canada geese have increased while birds such as the bearded tit, common whitethroat, red poll and mute swan are now low in numbers.

5 Retrace your steps up the embankment after any refreshment and turn right towards the Humber Bridge with eventually the working tile works on your right. Continue under the bridge back to your starting point.

PLACES OF INTEREST NEARBY

The *Humber Bridge* may be no longer the world's largest single-span suspension bridge, but it is magnificent nevertheless. It is over a mile long between the piers and was the first bridge of its kind to have its towers built of reinforced concrete instead of steel. It was begun in 1972 and opened in 1981. There is a walkway across with another Country Park and Information Centre on the northern bank.

St Peter's Church at Beck Hill is really two churches. One, old St Peter's with its 70 foot high Saxon tower remains one of the most remarkable examples of Saxon architecture in England. Made redundant in 1972 it is now under the guardianship of English Heritage and has undergone an extensive scheme of repair. The other church, the 13th Century, *St Mary's* only 150 yards away is also well worth a visit.

BRIGG'S RIVERSIDE

An unusual walk starting from the pedestrianised precinct in the middle of the interesting market town of Brigg and following the waterside of the Ancholme River for almost the whole of the route. For much of the way it is a peaceful scene disturbed only occasionally by a passing pleasure craft, inward or outward bound.

The River Ancholme at Brigg.

An ancient river crossing of the Ancholme, Brigg was first recorded in 1235 as Glanford Bridge. Clearly, however, it was an important site much earlier for a boat dating back to the late Bronze Age (circa 1000 BC), over 48 feet long and over 5 feet wide, scooped out of a single oak tree and capable of carrying 50 men, was found in 1886 during excavations for the construction of the gas works. This rare treasure was sent to Hull Museum but unfortunately was destroyed during the bombing of that city during the Second World War. In 1884 a causeway constructed out of huge oak logs set on a layer of oak, hazel and yew boughs was found in a bed of clay by the brickyard. An oak raft some

17

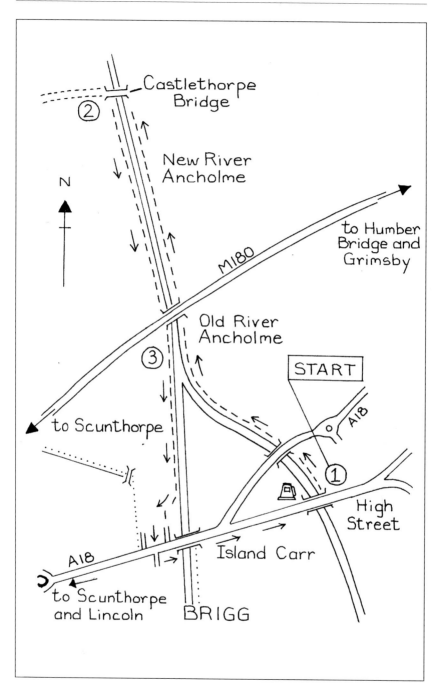

40 feet long was also discovered and there is a model of this in the museum at Lincoln. Recently, an environmental body, Enventure Northern, has awarded £40,000 to a scheme to restore the wetland banks of the River Ancholme at Brigg. The object is to boost the river's population of otters, kingfishers, moorhens and coots.

The Brocklesby Ox pub seen en route to the County Bridge recalls a famous Lincolnshire beast of more recent times, about 200 years ago, supposedly weighing 464 stones and standing 5 feet 6 inches tall. The Buttercross, once the town hall, is at the end of the market place (market days Thursday and Saturday) and is now an attractive tourist information centre. A pub in Bigby Street, with the unique name of The Dying Gladiator, has an appropriately gory sign. The Angel, in the market place, was once an old coaching inn but has now been very imaginatively converted into offices for North Lincolnshire Council. There were once 23 inns in town but many have now gone out of existence. A spring at nearby Castlethorpe was found to be ideal for brewing beer and a brewery was established in 1837 by A.M. and E. Sergeant. The renowned Dolphin ale won first prize at a Brewers Exhibition in London and it was a favourite pint for many years until the brewery finally closed in 1967.

Julie Hallas at the White Hart has a Mansfield real ale pub with lots of polished wood, carpeted floors and low beams. There are a number of interesting prints, some from Vanity Fair, and old photographs of the town. Woodpecker Cider, Scrumpy Jack Cider, Mansfield Bitter, Old Bailey Strong Bitter, Forster's Australian Beer and Ridings Bitter are served. Bar meals are available at normal times. There are ten picnic tables pleasantly situated on a riverside patio.

Telephone: 01652 654887.

- **HOW TO GET THERE:** Brigg lies on the A18(T) road east of Scunthorpe, or, on the A15 from Lincoln, via Redbourne, it is 4 miles beyond Hibaldstow. The starting place is from the County Bridge, Bridge Street, at the end of the Market Place.
- **PARKING:** There is ample free parking in town in the vicinity of the market place. The licensee of the White Hart in Bridge Street has kindly given permission to park in their car park if you intend using the pub before or after your walk.
- **LENGTH OF THE WALK:** 2¾ miles. Map: OS Landranger 112 Scunthorpe and surrounding area (GR 999072).

The view from Town Bridge.

THE WALK

1 From the County Bridge go down to the waterside path with the White Hart on your left across the Old River Ancholme and the former lemon curd factory on your right. At the turn of the century Spring's lemon curd was famous throughout the country, pronounced by many as the best lemon curd to be found in England. This explains the stone plaque still displayed on the wall at the end of the building. Walk under the new road bridge of Ancholme Way and continue along the tow path past the line of moored boats. Go below the noisy M180 motorway and proceed along the wide track for just over ½ mile. The odd surface here was created by dumping spoil from dredging onto the bank and it has only recently been properly levelled. This dredging was done in 1998 for the first time in 30 years and is unlikely to happen again for a very long time. On reaching the curious Castlethorpe Bridge climb the steep slope and cross the bridge.

2 Turn left down the embankment to follow the other bank after looking at the sweep of the escarpment leading on to the Humber. Walk back towards Brigg on this signposted and clear riverside path over Stewardship land that will be available for public access at least until 2006. The Ancholme is now on your left.

3 On reaching the M180 bridge once more continue forward on the same path beyond the river divide between the Old and the New Ancholme. At the very end of the present footway (it may be extended as the estate develops) turn right down the embankment into the attractive new housing development. This was the site of the Yarborough Oil Mill where raw sugar from Cuba was discharged after being transhipped into barges that could carry up to 60 tons. It was not the only industry in Brigg. Once there were four oil-seed crushing mills producing cattle cake within a mile of the market place. And another industry that sprang up here was the dressing of rabbit skins – by 1835 Brigg led the whole country with a special breed of silver grey rabbit! After only a few yards turn left up to the main road. Cross the road with care and turn left along Bridge Street back to your starting place.

PLACES OF INTEREST NEARBY

Boat trips can be taken from the moorings opposite the White Hart upstream as far as Brandy Wharf. Telephone 01724 851157 for details (between 6 pm and 9 pm). *Wrawby Post Mill* (which can be seen from the walk) is the last working postmill in the north of England. Stone-ground flour can be bought here. It is situated 1 mile off the A18 north-east of Brigg. Telephone: 01652 653699 (admission charge). *Normanby Hall Country Park* is 4 miles north of Scunthorpe on the B1430, with 300 acres of parkland, deer herds, ducks and peacocks. Telephone: 01724 720588.

TETNEY LOCK

A varied and interesting walk over level ground, starting and finishing alongside the long-abandoned Louth Canal. Newton Marsh Lane is then followed to a Humberside embankment path overlooking the shipping lane, the marsh and nature reserve with Haile Sand Fort out in the channel.

The Louth Navigation.

The canal actually gave birth to the Crown and Anchor inn at Tetney Lock for it was built expressly to supply the needs of the Irish navvies and to serve shipping. The canal scheme was proposed as far back as 1760 and the Act of Parliament for the cutting of the canal from Tetney Haven to Louth was passed in 1763. Within four years the first section from Tetney to Firebeacon was completed and another inn, 'The Ship', was opened. Though no longer an inn it still stands as part of an old warehouse on the bank 4 miles up the canal, just beyond Covenham Reservoir. For many years the innkeeper at Tetney Lock also operated a wharf and warehouses and he was described as a 'wharfinger and victualler'. Business was good in those early days, only declining as canal traffic dwindled, until it was finally abandoned in 1924. This was also a smugglers' coast and few ships sailed from Tetney Haven, Saltfleet or Grainthorpe without a bale or two of illicit wool in the hold. The Humber has vast, open sandy beaches where in good weather boats could run up out of the water or alternatively, casks or barrels could be thrown overboard to float gently ashore on the rising tide. Smuggling required the co-operation of many local people for storage, transport and distribution and a secret staircase was discovered at the Crown and Anchor during renovation work in the 1960s.

Spotless and warmly welcoming, this off-the-beaten-track canalside pub is under new management. There isn't a village at Tetney Lock and nowadays the canal traffic has disappeared but the Crown and Anchor offers hospitality to a diverse clientele consisting of members of the farming community, fishermen, walkers, wildfowlers, bird watchers and caravanners. The low-beamed parlour has a pool table and a darts board and at the side of the pub there is a pleasant, light and airy extension lounge bar with comfortable bench seating. Outside you will find picnic tables at the pub entrance and to the rear. There is a beer garden and a play area for children who are allowed in the pub until 8 pm. Dogs are not permitted in the lounge bar where food is served. Good value, simple bar meals are available. As for drinks, well-kept Bateman's Bitter on handpump and Bass Draught and Mild, Carling Black Label and Draught Guinness are on offer. The opening times are 12 noon until 4 pm and 7 pm until 11 pm except on Sunday when the pub closes at 10.30 pm.

Telephone: 01472 388291.

- **HOW TO GET THERE:** From the A1031 Grimsby-Mablethorpe road, turn off at Tetney for Tetney Lock (2 miles), or 3 miles north of Marshchapel to North Coates and then Tetney Lock.
- **PARKING:** On the roadside at Tetney Lock just beyond the former Coastguard Cottages by the waterside opposite the Old Chapel House. The start point is by the Coastguard cottages.
- **LENGTH OF THE WALK:** 5 miles. Map: OS Landranger 113 Grimsby and surrounding area (GR 342023).

THE WALK

1 From your parking place in front of the Coastguard Cottages (built 1842) above the Tetney Drain walk up to the bridge and turn left

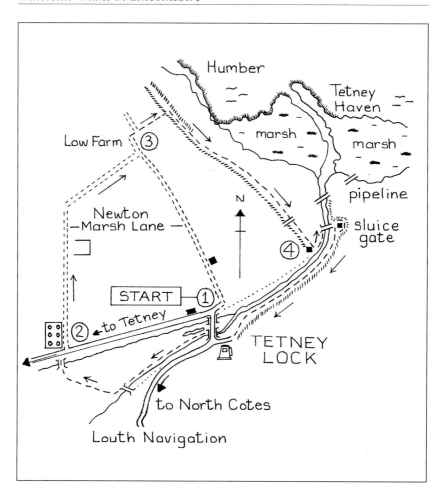

towards the Crown and Anchor. Before crossing the bridge over the Louth Navigation turn right with the canal now on your immediate left. Climb the stile with the fishing ponds and small caravan park on the right and follow the canal embankment path around the bends for 500 yards until you reach the bridge. Leave the canal bank here to turn right on a good track for about 450 yards. Turn right off the track on a signposted footpath with a small dyke on your right. Cross the footbridge to the road.

2 Go over the road leading to Tetney to follow the signposted footpath for Newton Marsh Lane, with the tank farm and its entrance

24

on your left. Continue up the lane past the sewage farm where the surfaced lane becomes a pleasant track. Turn right on this track all the way to the track junction where Low Farm is indicated. The farm and all its outbuildings have disappeared.

3 Turn left here over the curious block stile if the track is barred, otherwise continue along the track with the remaining hard standing of the former Low Farm on your left. Within a few yards turn right on a good track and where this track turns left continue straight on towards the Humber embankment with a prominent footpath signpost. Climb the embankment and turn right with the Humber and its shipping on the left. There are good views over the marsh one way and the distinct edge of the Wolds looking inland. The tower that may be seen over on the left is Grimsby Dock Tower. The marsh bird reserve forms an important feeding area in the mouth of the estuary and a large number of wildfowl and waders may be seen here on migration and in winter. Gulls roost on the sand bars in immense numbers and terns and skuas are frequent in autumn. Go under the oil pipeline with the incorrect warning notice for this is a definitive public right of way. About 3 miles off-shore lies the Tetney mono-buoy, the first to be installed in British waters. It is held in position by eight anchors and tankers are moored to it connected with floating hoses. Oil is pumped through the 36-inch pipeline that you walked under. The large storage tanks at the tank farm have a capacity of 2 million barrels. Oil is then transferred by a 14-mile pipeline to the refinery at South Killingholme.

4 Upon reaching the pill-box machine-gun post turn left down the track to the Sluice Gates. This area saw action during both world wars. Haile Sand Fort and the larger Bull Fort were built during the First World War at the vast cost of £2½ million. An anti-submarine net was stretched between the two forts. The first British Army casualties of the Second World War occurred here when a German mine-laying aeroplane machine-gunned the forts, which held garrisons of up to 200 men. Cross over the canal and turn right along the curving line of the embankment to a second machine-gun post. It is possible from here to gain a better view of the estuary and Spurn Head Lighthouse. Turn right by the machine-gun post to follow the pleasant embankment with the canal now on your right until you reach the inn. After refreshment turn right back over both bridges to your parking place.

Wartime defences above the marsh.

PLACES OF INTEREST NEARBY

In 1884 the Greenwich Meridian was established by international consent as the line from which longitude and time should be calculated, and at *Cleethorpes* a metal arrow set diagonally across the shore footpath is inscribed: 'This is the line of the Greenwich Meridian 0° 0° 0°'. A signpost indicates the distance to the North and South Poles and other places. It is tempting to put one foot in each hemisphere! Grid Ref 327067.

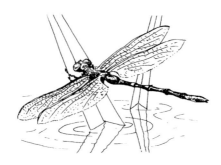

WILLINGHAM WOODS AND THE RIVER RASE

❧

Enjoy a gentle stroll at the very edge of the Wold, along the foot of the steep west facing scarp of the Lincolnshire Wolds and by the little River Rase. Tealby village, a Lincolnshire gem, is visited half way through the walk, offering opportunities for liquid or more substantial refreshment.

The lake at Willingham Woods.

Willingham Woods has a total area of about 2,700 acres and consists mainly of Scots and Corsican pine. It has been developed by the Forestry Commission on the sandy areas that were formerly warren and heath. The Forest Enterprise has done a splendid job in landscaping the picnic site with its ponds and providing a series of waymarked woodland walks. They are pleased for the public to be able to enjoy these walks providing that they keep to the rides, observe the Country Code and guard against fires. The term 'ride' has a special meaning in this context, for a ride is a wide avenue between standing trees, more

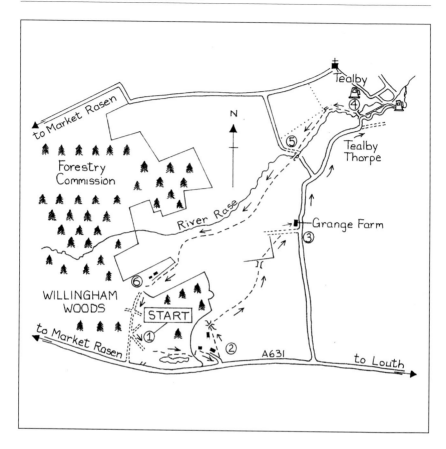

commonly known as a firebreak. The picnic site is a very convenient stopping-off place for families on their way to or from the coast. The little River Rase flows nearby and Tealby can record the sites of seven watermills along the stream and two millhouses may be seen even today. At Tealby Thorpe there is also a watermill that is open to the public from time to time. Paper Mill Lane, near Tealby church, indicates yet another use for which water power was formerly used.

One of the two public houses in Tealby, the rare thatched King's Head dates from 1357 (telephone: 01673 838347). The other equally interesting inn is The Old Barn Inn, situated in Cow Lane with Knights Templar connections (telephone: 01673 838304). Both welcome walkers and offer good value bar and restaurant meals. Tealby Tea Rooms in Front Street not only offer refreshment but also the possibility of hearing about the history of Tealby (telephone: 01673 838261).

- **HOW TO GET THERE:** Driving from Lincoln or Gainsborough on the A631 towards Louth continue straight on at Market Rasen crossroad traffic lights. The picnic site in Willingham Woods is on the left ½ mile beyond the end of the racecourse.
- **PARKING:** In the picnic site car park in Willingham Woods. Toilets.
- **LENGTH OF THE WALK:** 4½ miles. Map: OS Landranger 113 Grimsby and surrounding areas (GR 140884).

THE WALK

1 From the car park walk across the grass picnic area for about 100 yards with the main road over on your right, to arrive at a large footbridge over a tributary stream. Cross the bridge and on reaching the lake bear left by the fishing sign and remain here on the gravelled path. Bear left as far as the bungalow and the perimeter fence. Leave the wood here to turn right onto a tarmac square for vehicles and proceed forward keeping the mesh fence on your immediate left. Continue across the square and then the little lane that joins the main road. Just before reaching the junction turn left over a stile by a footpath signpost.

2 Walk diagonally left across the field aiming for the right-hand end of the storage building by the far left corner of this rough grazing area. Upon reaching the trees you will discover a stile, waymark and footbridge. Go over the bridge and aim for Grange Farm on a clear path with Tealby church tower to the left of your route. On reaching the stream coming in from the left (waymark) continue forward bearing slightly left until you reach another footbridge. Go over the bridge and proceed diagonally right across the field corner and continue on the same line until you come to the straight farm accommodation road leading to Grange Farm. Leave this track where it bends to the left and go straight forward with Grange Farm and buildings on your immediate left. Walk down the drive to the lane.

3 Turn left at the lane and continue on towards Tealby, ignoring the little lane on the left down to Tealby Thorpe. As you approach the village and some very attractive houses along Sandy Lane your return route is along a signposted footpath on the left by the second sharp bend in the road. However, the village itself is well worth exploring and stopping for refreshment. Do look at both fords, the rather splendid village hall and the church with its Tennyson connections.

4 Retrace your steps to the public footpath on Sandy Lane where there is a signpost, a stile and a footbridge with a handrail. Turn right (if you are coming from the village) and then left along the field edge with the stream on your immediate left. Go over a stile and after the abandoned sewage plant turn left again at a waymarked stile. Then proceed diagonally right across the grass field to a waymarked stile and ditchboard. Go over the double stile to walk straight forward with the hedge on your left. On reaching the stile cross onto the little lane.

5 Cross the footbridge over the infant River Rase and turn right on a signposted path to a stile. Follow the path round the field edge until you reach a footbridge on your right. Cross the bridge and proceed straight forward to an obvious signpost across the first field. On reaching this signpost walk forward towards the farm on the edge of Willingham Woods. Turn left over a stile to keep the farm buildings and then the farm houses on your immediate right until you reach a stile in the extreme right-hand corner of the field.

6 Continue down the farm drive to turn left on a good Forestry Commission track. At the track crossroads continue straight forward until you are almost in sight of the main road and then bear left on a waymarked path to the car park. The post is an orienteering control post and here you are following yellow and red route markers for the few yards back to the parking and picnic area.

PLACES OF INTEREST NEARBY

Hill House (formerly Horse World), at Sand Lane, Osgodby, Market Rasen (telephone: 01673 843407), has horses and ponies, a pets' corner, horses and cart rides, an owl and bird of prey sanctuary, and a cafeteria.

The Viking Way long distance recreational path follows the edge of the Wold hereabouts and passes through Tealby village and across the ford after coming down from Walesby Top Church (the *Ramblers' Church*) with its unique stained glass window of walkers and cyclists in the countryside. The church is always open. Footpath access only, but wonderful views.

WALK 6
HUTTOFT AND MOGG'S EYE

A remarkably varied walk along a lonely stretch of seashore which was once a smugglers' paradise, this also takes in a splendid range of sand dunes and an esplanade, a disused railway line that is fast becoming a nature reserve and a long green lane.

The green lane leading to Mogg's Eye sandhills.

Man-made sea defences protect this section of the Lincolnshire coast from twice-daily inundation by the sea. Occasionally, as in 1953 and to a lesser extent in 1978, these sea defences prove inadequate to prevent flooding by exceptional tide levels or storm surges. The sea level has been gradually rising since the end of the last Ice Age. Along this coast sometimes at neap tides stumps of trees may be seen which belong to a submerged prehistoric forest of about 4,500 years ago. A long bank built by the Romans to protect the land from the sea reached almost to this place, all the way from the River Welland beyond Boston. As you walk you will readily believe that these quiet shores and mysterious creeks and marshes were once a smugglers' paradise. Over the sea lay

31

Holland, the greatest producer of gin in Europe. So frequently was this spirit, generally known as Hollands, loaded and distributed in Lincolnshire that it gave the name to the village of New Holland, further up the coast on the south bank of the Humber. Goods commanding the highest duty were the obvious choice for smuggling and these were gin, brandy and tobacco. Excise officers once tracked a cargo that had been landed at Huttoft and 730 pounds of tobacco was seized. This haul was locked up at the Monson Arms in Lincoln where it was promptly stolen again. Sometimes goods were hidden in the sand dunes for collection later and some years ago boys playing on the beach found an old hog of tobacco. Excise officers were sometimes bribed and others met a nasty end. A skeleton discovered in the brickwork of the Vine Inn at Skegness had the royal insignia brass buttons still intact.

Members of the public are welcome at the clubhouse of the Sandilands Golf Club towards the beginning of the walk. It is a pleasant building and a good range of draught beers, lager and cider is served. There is a very reasonably priced menu and food is available all day. Telephone: 01507 441432.

- **HOW TO GET THERE:** From the A52 Mablethorpe-Skegness road turn east onto Sea Lane just under a mile north of Huttoft village.
- **PARKING:** On meeting the Sea Bank at the end of Sea Lane go straight ahead on the good concrete track to the coast. Beware the steep rise on meeting the sand dunes and turn right immediately onto the large concrete car park.
- **LENGTH OF THE WALK:** 7½ easy miles. This may be shortened to 6 miles although it would be a pity to do so. Map: OS Landranger 122 Skegness and surrounding area (GR 541786).

THE WALK

1 From the large car park turn left (north) towards Sutton-on-Sea either along the sea wall or the beach with the sea on your right and the golf course on the left. Continue for 1¼ miles. Turn left down the steps by the toilets and then left through the golf course car park with the club house on the left.

2 Cross the road to the footpath signpost and turn right behind the house to follow the clearly marked public footpath for 100 yards as far as the dyke and footbridge. A public footpath continues across the

32

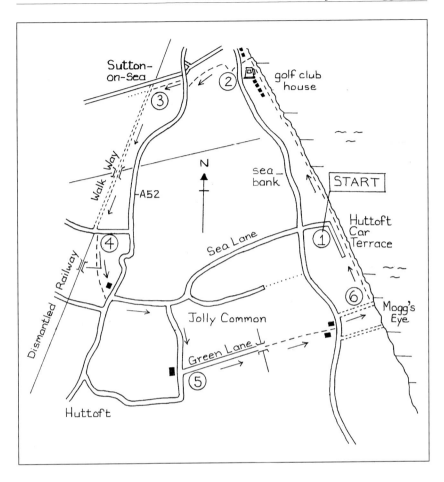

bridge but do not cross. Turn left with the dyke on your immediate right until you reach the wide grass entry of the path to the main road. Turn right for 100 yards and then left on the signposted footpath by the 40 mph signpost. Continue along this path until you reach the line of the old railway.

3 Turn left along the Sutton Branch Line Conservation Area and continue for 2¼ miles until you reach Crawcross Lane, crossing the wide Boy Grift Drain en route.

4 Cross the lane and go straight forward through the wooden fieldgate. Walk diagonally left to the bend in the dyke. Continue

The route at Point 3 of the walk.

forward with the dyke on your left to the end of the field where the dyke turns right. There should be a footbridge here but if it is not in place follow the dyke round to the field edge on the right where there is an old railway bridge. Cross the bridge and turn left on the other side of the dyke. On reaching the point where you would have crossed by the footbridge go through the wide gap in the hedge. Walk diagonally left across the field with The Grange and its out-buildings on your left. Walk towards the junction of the A52 and Sea Lane with its telephone box, aiming slightly to the right of the junction. It is signposted here 'To the Sea'. Walk up Sea Lane for ½ mile. For the SHORT CUT, carry straight on along Sea Lane back to the car park. Otherwise turn right by the sharp bend at the first junction for Jolly Common with Oakwell Farm on your right.

5   After ½ mile along this lane just before reaching Eastfield Farm on the right turn left down a wide green lane with a wartime bunker on the left. Upon reaching the bridge continue straight forward towards Bank House and its farm buildings. Keep the barn on your right. There is a stile here and a waymark. Walk through the farm entrance up the steep bank leading to Roman Bank. The public footpath here is actually on the left by the council house. Turn left along Roman Bank

The beach by Huttoft Car Terrace.

for 120 yards and then right up an unsurfaced green lane indicating a public footpath to the sea.

6 On reaching Mogg's Eye turn left along the shore for 900 yards back to Huttoft Car Terrace.

PLACES OF INTEREST NEARBY

The *Anderby Drainage Museum* at Anderby Creek is open alternate Sundays from 12th April until 27th September. Telephone: 01754 871594. *Hardy's Animal Farm*, Anchor Lane, Ingoldmells, opens Easter to the beginning of October. Telephone: 01754 872267. Admission charge. The *Skegness Natureland Seal Sanctuary* on North Parade, Skegness is open daily November to March, 10 am until 4 pm. Telephone: 01754 764345.

MARTON AND THE RIVER TRENT

A walk that offers unexpected and panoramic views over the River Trent into Nottinghamshire from the top of a small 'cliff'. The wide sweep of the marsh embankment on the outward route is surprisingly remote, except perhaps during a match in the fishing season! The 18th century Gate Burton Hall may be seen from the walk and nearer to the river, a folly known as Burton Chateau.

The River Trent at Marton.

History is all around you on this walk. Norsemen wintered at nearby Torksey where they constructed a temporary fort and when their policy changed from raids for plunder to permanent settlement, their riverside camp at Gainsborough became the headquarters for the conquest of England by King Swein of Denmark and his sons in 1013 to 1016. The Aegir or tidal bore may be seen on this stretch of the River Trent. It occurs during the March spring tides and the September equinox. It was so named by early Scandinavian settlers after their river god, Oegir. Part of the route is along an old Roman road, Littleborough Lane, and

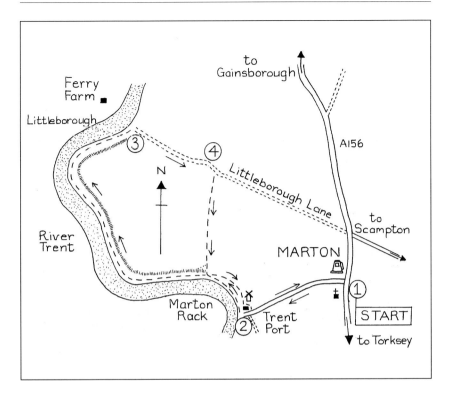

a Roman milestone found in Bailgate, Lincoln recorded the distance of 14 miles to Segelocum (now Littleborough). The Emperor Hadrian is reputed to have ordered the building of the river crossing and there was a Roman fort on the cliff to guard it. King Harold of England and his house carls also force-marched this way down the Roman road now known as Tillbridge Lane on their way to fight William of Normandy in 1066, immediately after they had defeated Harald Hardrada at the Battle of Stamford Bridge. What a march that must have been and your walk takes you to where they would have crossed the river. Even the main road to Gainsborough has its memories. Oliver Cromwell here won a small but desperate victory on 28th July 1643 that proved his reputation as a superb cavalry commander. In an attempt to relieve the Gainsborough garrison besieged by Royalist forces, he defeated the young General Cavendish, a godson of Charles Stuart, but then had to retreat when the Earl of Norwich approached the town with overwhelming forces. Cromwell fought a masterly rearguard action, halting and facing his pursuers no less than nine times along this road.

37

The jetty at Trent Port.

The Ingleby Arms is a small country pub with a very pleasant grassed area at the rear. A good selection of beers, stouts and lagers are available and you will be made most welcome. However, food is not served in the establishment, so should you need a meal before or after your walk, the Hume Arms at Torksey is just 2 miles down the road towards Saxilby. There you will find a wide range of both bar and restaurant meals.

Telephone: Hume Arms 01427 718594.

- **HOW TO GET THERE:** Marton is situated on the A156 some 5 miles south of Gainsborough. Alternatively Marton can be reached by driving 9 straight miles down the A1500 Roman Road from Scampton crossroads.
- **PARKING:** In the Ingleby Arms car park by kind permission of the landlord if you intend to use the pub before or after your walk. Alternatively, parking may be found off the main road on Trent Port Lane by the playing field on the left just beyond the church.
- **LENGTH OF THE WALK:** 3 miles. Map: OS Landranger 121 Lincoln and surrounding area (GR 840818).

THE WALK

1 From the Ingleby Arms car park turn right towards the church and right again down Trent Port Lane with the cross, the church and the village playing field over on your left. Continue along this pleasant lane for 700 yards until you reach Trent Port. There was once a wharf, a malthouse and a working mill at Trent Port in the days of flourishing river traffic but today only the old mill remains.

2 Walk straight on almost to the water's edge to turn right through the new gateway at the side of the field gate. Should this route be too wet due to a high tide, walk up the path by the mill instead and on coming to the steps by the second stile come back down to the marsh. On the riverside path continue forward at the base of the cliff and after about 300 yards go through the gate onto the embankment on the marsh. Continue forward in a wide loop of 1¼ miles until you come to the historic Littleborough Lane with the hamlet of Littleborough across the river.

3 Turn right on this very ancient unsurfaced green lane and former Roman road for 700 yards. As the lane begins to ascend turn right on the signposted footpath to climb the stile and walk up the steep bank to the top of the cliff. Continue along the cliff-edge path that offers some fine views to the countryside above Marton village and into Nottinghamshire. It is only some ten to fifteen yards above the path you used across the marsh but it appears to be much higher at times. Continue to keep the river on your right over various stiles until you reach the old mill once more.

4 From the old mill follow the track down to Trent Port to turn left back along the lane into Marton village. Upon your return it is worth examining the herringbone coursing in the tower of St Margaret's church for it is either very clearly Norman or late Saxon work right up to the bell chamber. The war memorial in the corner of the churchyard is said to have once been an old market cross.

PLACES OF INTEREST NEARBY

Torksey Leisure Cruises at Torksey Lock (telephone: 01427 880609) are open throughout the year for Sunday lunch cruises. *Gainsborough Old Hall* in Parnell Street, Gainsborough (telephone: 01427 612669) is a perfectly preserved medieval manor house with original kitchens and magnificent Great Hall. Admission charge.

LINCOLN AND THE FOSSDYKE

An attractive riverside inn, the Fossdyke Roman Canal with good views of Lincoln Cathedral set high upon its hill, and a peaceful bridlepath along the Catchwater Drain enhance this delightful walk.

The junction of Catchwater Drain and the Fossdyke.

The Romans were great civil engineers who not only built a whole new system of roads, forts and towns but also dug waterways to link river routes and improve drainage. The Fossdyke, still in use today as a navigable canal, links Brayford Pool in Lincoln with the River Trent at Torksey. At one time no less a person than the Bishop of Lincoln was responsible for seeing that the Fossdyke Canal was kept open so that craft could pass to and fro. Silting of this waterway was one of the reasons given for the decline in Lincoln's trade. The Fossdyke was Crown Property until the visit of James I to Lincoln in 1617 when the Mayor and Corporation received this royal but doubtful gift. In 1846 when the railway companies became the owners of both the Fossdyke and the Witham Navigation, water trade declined. During this century

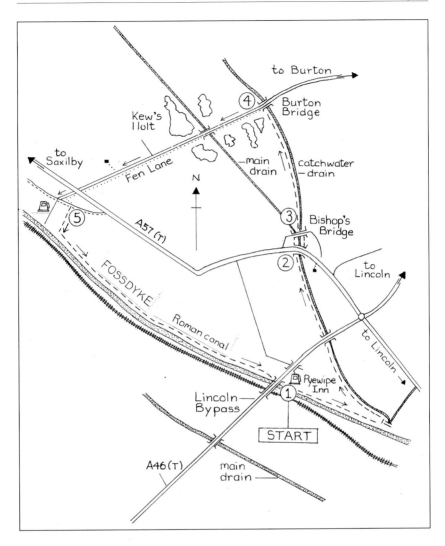

the main traffic was imported goods coming by barge from Hull docks to Lincoln. Almost all the vessels working on the Fossdyke were unpowered until the 1930s when the introduction of diesel engined craft brought a vast change in the lifestyle of the crews. Until then a barge skipper invariably used the forces of nature to make the voyage from Hull to Lincoln. Without a fair wind, a canvas or leather 'seal' was fitted to a haulier's shoulders and the barge was then pulled from the towpath. There were horses for hire at Torksey but the fee had to be paid out of the captain's two-thirds share of the freight money. The other third went to the owner of the boat.

The Pyewipe Inn is under new ownership and after a total refurbishment is now a very pleasant free house offering a range of real ale in an attractive riverside situation. It is open from 11 am until 11 pm and meals are available all day. Well behaved dogs are permitted in the grounds.

Telephone: 01522 521315.

- **HOW TO GET THERE:** Proceeding towards Saxilby from Lincoln on the A57(T) turn left on a signposted track ½ mile beyond the bypass roundabout. Coming towards Lincoln on the A57(T) turn right on the signposted track ¾ mile beyond the Burton T junction. The Pyewipe Inn is ¾ mile up this track.
- **PARKING:** Ample parking in the inn car park (by kind permission of the landlord).
- **LENGTH OF THE WALK:** 4½ miles. Map: OS Landranger 121 Lincoln and surrounding area (GR 949724).

THE WALK

1 Leaving the inn car park climb the embankment of the Fossdyke and turn left towards Lincoln. Barges carrying timber to Lincoln often queued along here as far as the Pyewipe, particularly in the early summer months after ships bringing timber to Hull had been released from the ice in the Baltic. A wait of six weeks was not uncommon at that time. On arriving at the attractive old bridge after 600 yards do not cross but turn left to a stile and proceed along another embankment with the Catchwater Drain on your immediate right. Pass below the bypass and continue to Bishop's Bridge with Waves Farm over on the left.

2 Cross the road with care to turn right over the bridge. Then turn left with the drain on your immediate left for a few yards to the old road.

3 Cross the old road and turn left over the little bridge. Immediately turn right on the signposted path indicating 'Burton Bridge ½ mile'. The Catchwater Drain is again on your right and the Main Drain over on the left.

4 On reaching Burton Bridge turn left down Fen Lane with Kew's Holt on the right. Cross the busy main road and walk up the drive leading

The Pyewipe Inn on the Fossdyke.

to Woodcock's. Do not enter but turn left on the old main road for about 150 yards.

5 Turn right on a signposted fenced footpath leading back to the Fossdyke. Skipper John Musgrave loaded his barge at Lincoln for Hull just after Christmas 1939 and the cargo finally reached Hull on the last day of March, 1940. He had spent all that time iced in on the Fossdyke. A tug failed to make any impression on the ice and badly damaged her plates in the attempt. Climb the bank and turn left along the towpath for 1¼ miles back to the Pyewipe Inn.

PLACES OF INTEREST NEARBY

Ellis Mill, Mill Road, can be seen from the walk. It is a working mill and flour is for sale. Open May to September, Saturday and Sunday, 2 pm to 6 pm. Telephone: 01522 523870.

Attractions in Lincoln itself include the *Castle* and *Cathedral*. The *Sir Joseph Banks Conservatory*, The Lawn, Union Road (telephone: 01522 560306) is a tropical conservatory commemorating the species collected by Sir Joseph Banks on Cook's voyage to Australia. Nearby, the *John Dawber Garden* is a formal walled garden with species depicting Lincoln's partnership with worldwide cities.

WALK 9

DONINGTON ON BAIN

A lovely peaceful walk over a stretch of the Wolds above Donington on Bain with some wonderful views. The medieval village site of Biscathorpe is passed and the infant River Bain is followed in the valley.

The ford at Biscathorpe.

Donington on Bain, where this walk begins, is a large and thriving village which is well known on the other side of the world. A memorial in the church commemorates Captain Matthew Flinders RN (1774 - 1814), the first man to circumnavigate Australia. Just along the Bain valley is the remote Wolds hamlet of Biscathorpe which is within one of the main concentrations of 'lost' villages in Lincolnshire. Apart from Biscathorpe itself, there are East and West Wykeham, Calcethorpe and South Cadeby within a mile or so of each other. The theory of ley lines asserts that the whole of Britain is criss-crossed with alignments of ancient sites that form uncanny but undeniably straight lines. A line drawn from Biscathorpe Church to Sandilands Church at Sutton on Sea will cover a crossroads north-west of Withcall, old moats at Tathwell

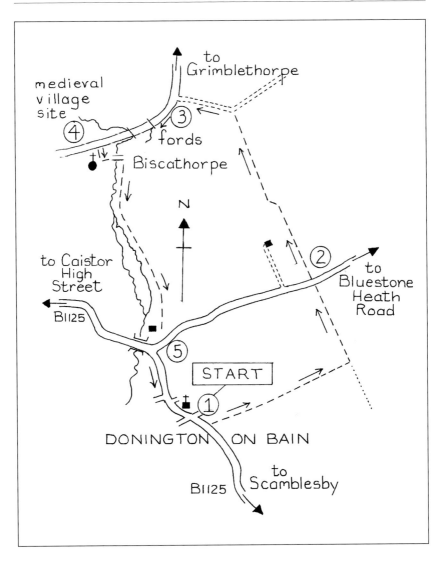

to Grimblethorpe

medieval village site

③

④

fords

Biscathorpe

N

to Caistor High Street

B1125

②

to Bluestone Heath Road

⑤

START

①

DONINGTON ON BAIN

to Scamblesby

B1125

Cottage and Gillwood's Grange, and an ancient earthwork at Withern. The pre-Christian inhabitants of these islands, especially those of Celtic extraction regarded the earth herself as a living creature whose powers could be tapped for good or evil. Later Christian churches were deliberately built on ancient pagan religious sites to encourage converts to worship the new God on the very spot where they formally worshipped the old ones. These nationwide strange alignments seem to be based on standing stones, standing water and sites of apparent religious significance. However, the most prominent feature you will notice today is the Belmont television mast, which dominates the countryside above Donington on Bain. This was built in 1964 by the Independent Television Authority for joint use with the BBC and was the second tallest mast in Europe at the time. It transmits to an area from Bridlington and Doncaster in the north to as far as March in the south.

The 18th century Black Horse pub is a real ale inn under the enthusiastic management of Tony and Janine Pacey. The lounge bar has old beams, an open fire in season and three attractive inglenooks. The establishment has been transformed in recent years and now offers en suite accommodation. Bar meals are available and there is a restaurant. A goodly range of drinks are on offer. The Viking Way long distance recreational path actually passes the door so walkers are well catered for. Tony asks though that muddy footwear is left outside.

Telephone: 01507 343640.

- **HOW TO GET THERE:** Turn southwards off the A157 Louth-Lincoln Road half way between Burgh on Bain and Hainton (1½ to 2 miles) onto Caistor High Street (B1125) aiming for the Donington on Bain radio mast that dominates the countryside for miles around. After 1½ miles leave the High Street and turn down the hill to Donington on Bain in the valley below.
- **PARKING:** In the Black Horse car park by kind permission of the landlord.
- **LENGTH OF THE WALK:** 4½ miles. Map: OS Landranger 122 Skegness and surrounding area (GR 237829).

THE WALK

1 Turn left on leaving the car park to walk down the Main Street for about 200 yards. Turn left over a stile on a signposted public footpath opposite Meadowcroft. Continue forward with the hedge and ditch on your immediate right. For a few yards it is often muddy here at the base of the slope. Continue straight uphill on a good track passing through beautiful plantations with splendid views. At the top of the hill turn left at a cross tracks to follow a well defined bridleway as far as Welsdale Road.

2 Cross the lane and continue along the bridleway. It initially keeps to headlands with the hedges and bushes to the left and then follows a ridge with open land on either side with fine views of the River Bain down on the left. The hedge line is picked up to the left again and 200 yards on, at a three-way finger post, go diagonally left along the farm accommodation road leading down to Grange Farm hidden in the valley on the right. It is about 500 yards to the lane.

3 Turn left on meeting the lane down into Biscathorpe. There are two fords at the bottom - one for the young River Bain and the other for a tributary stream. The 'lost' village site is on your right by the tributary stream. Continue along this little lane until you are almost level with the cottage.

4 Turn left over the grass with the garden, the cottage and the church on your right until you reach the field corner. Cross the stile and turn left down the fenced track to the bridge and stile. Turn right with the River Bain and Biscathorpe Lake on your right and continue over various stiles for almost a mile.

5 On reaching the lane turn right and then left back into the village. The waters of Biscathorpe Lake feed down to the mill at Donington on Bain where, it is said, the ghost of a murdered girl may sometimes be seen gliding across the water. The picturesque water mill is on your right here but it is best viewed from the road bridge on the right.

PLACES OF INTEREST NEARBY
Benniworth House Farm at Donington on Bain is a Countryside Commission Access Site (GR 230830). Ten hectares of historic meadows lying alongside the meandering River Bain and easily reached from the village make it ideal for exploring and a riverside picnic. These meadows also form a valuable nature reserve.

THE ROMAN CAR DYKE

This walk, with marvellously contrasting views, is along one of the best preserved sections of the Roman Car Dyke on the very edge of the Fen indicating, even today, what great civil engineers the Romans must have been. Woodland walks are rare in much of Lincolnshire but this one also introduces you to the delights of Potterhanworth Wood.

Car Dyke, the Roman canal.

There are wonderful views on this walk from the footpath at the edge of Neville Wood looking over the rolling fields to the church and the village of Potterhanworth Booths and then over miles and miles of the rich black soil of the Fen stretching towards Wasps Nest, Sot's Hole and the sugar beet factory at Bardney. The 'Booths' of the hamlet's name means shelter, initially temporary, on land that had dried out after the winter and was available for summer pasture. It was the Romans, during their 350 years' effective occupation of Lincolnshire, who first made serious attempts to drain the Fen and check flooding. They dug a banked canal, the Car Dyke, to catch and carry off the flood waters

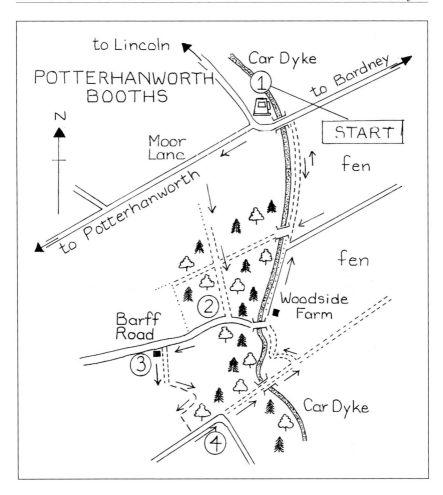

from the higher ground. It extends from the Witham just south of Lincoln to Waterbeach in Cambridgeshire and is still traceable along most of its 76 miles. For much of its route it was carefully engineered to skirt the Fen edge, joining the Rivers Slea, Glen, Welland and Nene. Although a few sections have been filled in and levelled others still function as part of the present-day drainage system. Some historians believe that the Dyke was unlikely to have ever been a continuous navigable channel yet it certainly was used for some traffic. Henry Penn, bell-founder of Peterborough, cast a bell, *Great Tom of Lincoln*, in 1717 and it was sent (all 4½ tons of it) on a raft down the Car Dyke to Lincoln Cathedral.

The Plough is an attractive and well-kept country pub under new management serving John Smith's and Ruddocks County beer and, of course, varying guest beers. There is a sunny lounge bar where a range of reasonably priced bar meals are available. Telephone: 01522 794798.

- **HOW TO GET THERE:** Potterhanworth Booths is on the Lincoln to Bardney B1190 road, 6½ miles south-east out of Lincoln via Washingborough.
- **PARKING:** At the Plough Inn (by kind permission of the landlord).
- **LENGTH OF THE WALK:** 4 miles, with a shorter alternative of 2 miles. Map: OS Landranger 121 Lincoln and surrounding area (GR 075680).

THE WALK

1 From the pub car park walk round the bend of the road to the left towards Bardney. Cross the road bridge and the road with care to turn right down the embankment path with the Car Dyke on your immediate right. Continue for 1,100 yards until you meet the good footbridge with handrail and a footpath signpost.

2 Cross the bridge (the steps leading down may be slippy) and go through the kissing gate into Potterhanworth Wood. The attractive path soon widens into a forest ride and after a short distance you will find a hard core track along the right of the ride. After some 500 yards you will come to a track cross-roads and a four-fingered public footpath signpost. Turn left down the main drive until you reach another kissing gate and Barff Road ('Barff' means a ridge of higher land on the edge of the Fen). Turn right here down the road until you reach Barff Farm. However, the public footpath sign across the road on your left leads you into Burnt Wood and back again to the road in a U-shape. If you have plenty of time it is a pleasant little detour.

(For the shorter walk, simply turn left on reaching Barff Road to walk down to the Car Dyke and turn left along the Dyke back to your starting point.)

3 Turn left off the road by Barff Farm on a signposted footpath track that drops down into the valley. Turn left on reaching the hedgeline (signpost) and follow the field edge round with Neville Wood on your immediate left. Cross the little footbridge to Nocton Fen Lane, after looking across the rolling fields to Potterhanworth church and village. Turn left down the lane.

4   Where the lane turns sharp right to Wasp's Nest continue straight on down the unsurfaced track. Cross the bridge over the Car Dyke and continue along the green lane for 250 yards with the wonderful wide sweep of the Fen before you and Bardney in the distance. Turn left up to Woodside Farm buildings and then follow the embankment path with the Car Dyke on your left all the way back to the Bardney Road and well deserved refreshment at The Plough.

PLACES OF INTEREST NEARBY

Metheringham Airfield Visitor Centre, Westmoor Farm, Martin Moor, Metheringham (telephone: 01526 378270) has a fascinating exhibition of photographs and memorabilia which recall life on the Second World War airfield of RAF Metheringham. Open April to October, Saturday, Sunday and Bank Holidays, 12 noon until 5 pm. The *Timberland Pumping Station Visitor Centre* is at Walcott Bank, Tattershall Bridge, on the River Witham between Tattershall and Kirkstead Bridge. 'Tales of the River Bank' relates the history of Fen drainage in this area. Open from 1st May until the 31st October, Wednesday to Sunday, 2 pm to 5 pm, admission free. Telephone: 01526 345718.

THE OLD HORNCASTLE CANAL

A peaceful walk along an old canal embankment in the valley of the River Bain. You may well see a heron en route. There is also some grassland walking and two separate stretches along quiet roads.

Old locks on the Horncastle Canal.

The closing decades of the 18th century saw canal construction in many parts of England. In 1786 the Tattershall Canal was opened, linking Tattershall to the River Witham and later, after overcoming financial difficulties, it was extended to Horncastle by canalizing the River Bain in 1802. This meant that traffic could travel from Horncastle, via the canal and the River Witham to the Trent and the Humber in one direction and Boston and the Wash in the other. The total fall in the level over the 11 miles from Horncastle to the Witham was 84 feet and this was managed by 11 locks, one of which was at Kirkby on Bain and another at Haltham. Boats of up to 50 tons could travel on the canal with a maximum length of 72 feet. The main cargoes coming up to Horncastle were coal, fertilizer and general goods with farming produce supplying the outgoing traffic. Canal traffic gradually declined with the coming of the railway – the Boston to Lincoln railway opened in 1848 and the Horncastle to Kirkstead line in 1855. The last recorded cargo on the canal was in May 1878 – 31 tons of guano from Boston to Horncastle! Today the canal is disused but makes a pleasant companion for a walk taking in the villages of Kirkby on Bain and Haltham. The Marmion Arms at Haltham takes its name from the ancient family of the King's Champions, an honour bestowed upon Sir Robert Marmion by William the Conqueror in 1086. The present Queen's Champion, Colonel Sir John Dymoke, still resides in an estate close by. The Marmion coat of arms is displayed at the front of the pub which is believed to be the only timber-framed, wattle and daub, thatched property of its kind in Lincolnshire and possibly in the country. An old AA circular disc sign on the wall outside indicating the mileage to London is of interest.

The Marmion Arms is a friendly, welcoming hostelry ably run by two professionals, Rob Moon and Maureen Lindley with quality ales such as Adnam's Bitter, Mansfield Bitter, Old Bailey Strong Bitter, McEwan's Lager, Murphy's Stout and Scrumpy Jack Cider on offer. Mild beer is not served. An à la carte menu using fresh local produce complements the variety of traditional bar meals available including vegetarian meals and children's portions. Opening hours are 12 noon until 3 pm throughout the week and 7 pm until 11 pm Monday to Saturday with a 10.30 pm closing on Sunday. There is a very pleasant beer garden with picnic tables. Telephone: 01507 568326.

- **HOW TO GET THERE:** Haltham is 5 miles south of Horncastle on the A153 road to Sleaford.
- **PARKING:** In the large car park at the Marmion Arms, Haltham (by kind permission of the landlord).
- **LENGTH OF THE WALK:** 2¼ or 3½ miles. Map: OS Landranger 122 Skegness and surrounding area (GR 247637).

THE WALK

1 From the pub entrance walk down West Lane for 300 yards to turn right on a signposted footpath by the new bungalow towards the end of the cul-de-sac. Almost immediately turn left behind the houses to a stile and bridge and on to the embankment of the now disused Horncastle Canal with its stile and four-fingered direction post. Go straight across the lock and then the second bridge over the old course

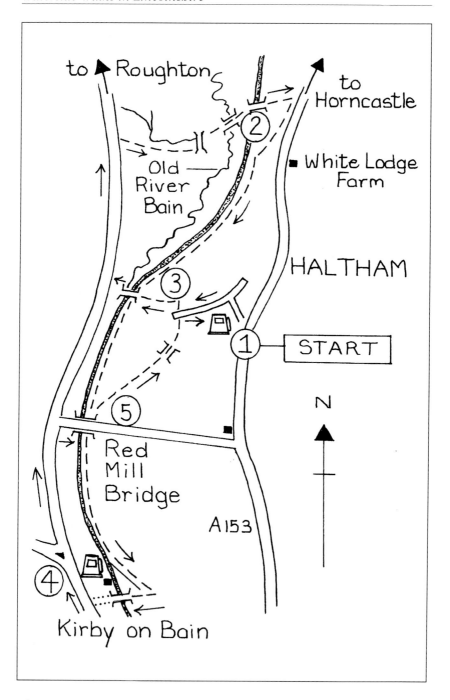

The Ebrington Arms at Kirkby on Bain.

of the River Bain and down to the lane. Turn right along the lane for 700 yards and then right off the lane on a signposted and clearly defined public footpath across to the hedge, where it becomes a headland path with the hedge on your immediate left. Cross the small footbridge through the hedge, then a bridge over the old River Bain and finally a much larger bridge over the Horncastle Canal.

2 The correct route goes across this rough pasture up beside the hedge on the left to the field corner by the roadside (signpost). Then turn diagonally right on a separate public footpath down the field to an old hedgeline and then the canal embankment. Walk along the embankment in a long curve until you meet the four-fingered direction post once again.

   For the shorter walk, turn left here down the embankment and return along West Lane to the Marmion Arms. This is 2¼ miles and should take about an hour.

3 For the longer walk continue along the embankment with the canal still on your right for 650 yards to Red Mill Bridge. Go directly across Rimes Lane and over the stile to continue along the embankment until you meet the fence. Go down the embankment here and continue forward with the fence/hedge on your immediate right, passing the curious stone blocks from the abandoned canal on the way. On reaching the hedgeline across your front do not cross the obvious stile but turn right to climb the stile at the side of the fieldgate and onto a track. Cross over the sleeper bridge with the weir upstream on the right.

4 Turn right on reaching the main road in Kirkby on Bain with the attractive Ebrington Arms on the right. Continue straight forward along the road back to Rimes Lane and Red Mill Bridge.

5 Turn right to the bridge and then left over the stile to proceed diagonally right across the field aiming for the Haltham farm buildings in the distance. Cross the culvert over the dyke and turn left round the field corner and on to a stile at the side of the house. Walk up to West Lane to turn right back to the Marmion Arms.

PLACES OF INTEREST NEARBY

The *Battle of Britain Memorial Flight* at RAF Coningsby includes the only Lancaster still flying in Britain. It is open Monday to Friday, 10 am to 5 pm. Telephone: 01526 344041. At the crossroads in Woodhall Spa can be found the *Dambusters Memorial*. Just south of Hallam is *Tattershall Castle*. This was restored at the beginning of the 20th century and is now in the hands of the National Trust. It is open from April to October. Telephone: 01526 342543.

WAINFLEET AND THE RIVER STEEPING

Wainfleet All Saints is an intriguing little market town on the River Steeping, no longer a port but set amid highly-productive reclaimed marshland. The walk begins by the 15th century Magdalen College School and follows the river's course to Crow's Bridge.

Crow's Bridge over the River Steeping.

A couple of thousand years ago this little salt-panning place on a navigable river with a safe haven sheltered from the North Sea gales was both a port and a meeting place of routes. The Romans called the port Vainona from the British word for a marsh and later they added the word 'fleet' to indicate a navigable creek. The Saxons and the Danes used Wainfleet and seven circular graves with smooth double linings of clay containing pottery, shells and pieces of bone were found in one barrow a century ago when the railway line was laid. The 'Green Hill' is another such barrow, crowned today with four trees and

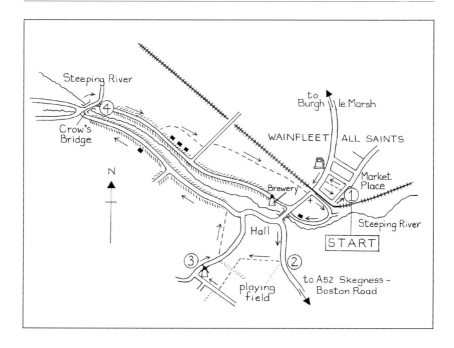

left intact in a meadow by Northolme Hall. Although Wainfleet is no longer a port the river still provides an important amenity and attraction. Named the Steeping River above the town it becomes Wainfleet Haven below it, although the stretch down to Gibraltar Point was called either Queen's Gowt or Wainfleet Clough. Land drainage in the 17th century led to the silting up of the river harbour and from then on Wainfleet's economy became centred on agriculture. The former windmill tower seen across the river, surmounted by the largest beer bottle in the county, is part of Bateman's Brewery, perhaps Lincolnshire's best known ale manufacturer. Just off the High Street you can find Barkham Street, named after Edmund Barkham who gave much property to the town before he died in 1732. This street, Wainfleet's most extraordinary feature, was built by the Governors of Bethlem Hospital (who owned a great deal of land in the county, including Wingland). It is a replica of a London street, closed to through traffic, designed to look like their other three-storeyed Victorian terraces erected by the Foundation in Southwark. A number of Bateman's pubs – The Red Lion, The Woolpack and the Royal Oak – may be found along the High Street, almost within sight of the brewery. The Angel is a John Smith's house so there is a wide choice of welcoming hostelries. The Royal Oak is a particularly friendly place and it is open from 11 am until 11 pm for much of the year. It also serves draught Guinness, cider and lagers and offers the kind of good bar meals that one often finds in rural market towns. Accommodation is available. The telephone number for the Royal Oak is 01754 880328.

- **HOW TO GET THERE:** Wainfleet All Saints is on the A52 Boston to Skegness road some 7 miles south of Skegness, or alternatively 9½ miles along the B1195 from Spilsby.
- **PARKING:** There is a car park in front of the Magdalen College building.
- **LENGTH OF THE WALK:** 3¼ miles. Map: OS Landranger 122 Skegness and surrounding area (GR 499589).

THE WALK

1 Straight across from the car park by the museum, cross the road and follow the narrow passageway down to the High Street. Turn left towards the railway crossing. Immediately after the crossing turn left down Church Lane and at the end right along Havenside with the river on your left and Bridge House on the right. Upon reaching Salem Bridge turn left at the road and left again down Boston Road for 350 yards.

2 Cross the road to follow a tarmac path around the bend to a footbridge and double footpath signpost, only a few yards beyond the 'Welcome to Wainfleet' sign. Go through the metal handgate and take the right-hand public footpath. Cross the line of trees and a footpath stile will then come into view. Aim across the grazing field to the white shed on the right where you will find a kissing gate and a waymark. Walk across the playing field to the prominent gap in the hedge with the fence on your right and continue straight forward to the lane. Turn right down St Michael's Lane, disregarding the overgrown public footpath with a signpost on the left. Turn right at the road junction by the old mill and continue along the road for about 300 yards.

3 At Half Penny Hill Cottage turn left off the road over the stile with a footpath signpost and continue on the path until you reach the road. Turn left along Haven Bank to follow the top of the bank with the river on your right for ¾ mile until you reach Crow's Bridge.

4 Turn right over the bridge and right again along the top of the

The old windmill, now part of Bateman's Brewery.

embankment with the river now on your immediate right and the lane below you on the left. Just before reaching the second house on the left leave the embankment and cross the road to follow the signposted footpath with a kissing gate and a dyke on the left. Go behind the houses and upon reaching the minor road turn left for a few yards. Turn right over an old footbridge with a new handrail to follow a narrow tarmac path. Cross two more footbridges and continue forward until you reach the main road with a new small estate on your left.

5 Upon reaching the main road turn left over the railway crossing and right down Silver Street with the railway now on your right. Continue on this street round the bend to your starting place.

PLACES OF INTEREST NEARBY

The *Gibraltar Point National Nature Reserve* is a reserve with a Visitor Centre, open from dawn to dusk throughout the year. Telephone: 01754 762677. In Wainfleet, the *Magdalen Museum* in St John's Street (telephone: 01754 881261) is open from Easter to the end of September, Tuesday and Thursday to Sunday, 1.30 pm to 4.30 pm. You can pre-book for an evening tour at 7 pm of *Bateman's Salem Bridge Brewery* by telephoning 01754 880317.

THE WASH AT WRANGLE

Easy walking on ancient and newer sea banks above the marsh at Wrangle and by rich arable fields brings distant views of the sea with ships often lying off in Boston Deeps. One can hardly find a more remote spot than your starting point, the Sailors Home and who on earth their customers were when it was a pub is difficult to comprehend!

The lonely track leading to the marsh.

Wrangle was quite an important place in the 13th and 14th centuries with a thriving Saturday market which served the surrounding district. In 1359 when Edward III was raising a navy to invade France, Wrangle was one of the 82 places in the kingdom requested to help. The village sent one ship and eight men, whereas Liverpool only provided one ship and five men. The church of St Mary and St Nicholas dating from the 13th century is a fine Marshland church with a wealth of 600 year old glass. John Reade of Wrangle Hall, merchant of the Staple of Calais and his wife, both of whom died in 1503, are portrayed in brass and below them are grouped 13 children. Sir John Reade, their great-

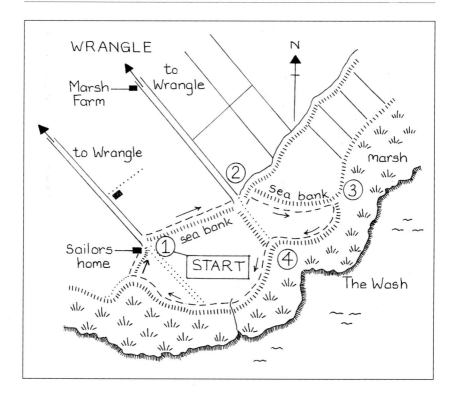

grandson, who died in 1626 has a high altar tomb with a melancholy tableau below of his children, some holding skulls. There are some unusual and grotesque gargoyles around the exterior of the church.

There were originally eight pubs in the parish. The Angel at Wrangle is an appropriately named archetypal low-beamed village pub situated directly opposite the splendid parish church right in the village centre. It is a pleasant John Smith's house serving the usual range of traditional, good value bar meals and popular with locals. Restaurant facilities are available.

Telephone: 01754 880324.

- **HOW TO GET THERE:** Wrangle village is on the A52, 8½ miles north of Boston. From the War Memorial cross by Wrangle church then drive down Church Lane and turn right onto Hall Lane End (not Hall Lane to the left). Take the next left and then the next left and at the end of the tarmac road you will find the Sailors Home on your right.
- **PARKING:** With care near the old sea bank on the grass verge of the

road leading to the Sailors Home but please do not block the entrance.

- **LENGTH OF THE WALK:** 3¼ miles. Maps: OS Landranger 131 Boston and surrounding area, 122 Skegness and surrounding area (GR 446491).

THE WALK

1 Do have a look at the notice board before you start. Then, from your starting point near the Sailors Home (not a home for elderly seamen but an old inn) on one of the lanes called Sea Lane, facing seaward, turn left along a signposted footpath on the top of an old sea bank. Continue for ¾ mile. The 'high' land is formed from silt banks deposited by the sea in ages past. These banks were occupied by medieval salt-makers who evaporated brine to make salt. As late as 1814 there was still a memory of Wrangle Haven coming to within ½ mile of the church.

2 Reach the end of a tarmac lane on your left (also called Sea Lane) with the aptly named Marsh Farm up the road on your left. Do not turn right immediately on the good track that is an extension of the lane but walk forward to follow the curving sea bank diagonally right.

Wrangle church.

Sailors Home.

3 Upon reaching the stile turn right on the outermost sea bank with the marsh on your immediate left. Continue until you meet the straight track leading back to Marsh Farm. People still go down to the marshes in September to gather samphire, for the foreshore provides ideal conditions for growth. Centuries ago samphire was burnt to provide ash which was an impure carbonate of soda for mixing with sand in the glass-making process. Today samphire is eaten as an asparagus-like starter for a meal, or for the real traditional Lincolnshire dish it needs to be pickled and eaten with stuffed chine or boiled bacon.

4 Continue on the outermost bank past the straight track leading to the Sailors Home. Turn right off the embankment onto another old sea bank, leading round to the right and your starting place by the Sailors Home.

PLACES OF INTEREST NEARBY

At Boston, the tower of St Botolph's church, known locally as *Boston Stump*, soars to 272 feet. It is possible for members of the public to climb the tower and there is quite a view. In the *Guildhall Museum* the cells where the Pilgrim Fathers were imprisoned in 1607 may be seen. The *Pilgrims' Memorial* is at Haven Country Park, Fishtoft, Boston (GR 374402).

WALK 14

HAVERHOLME AND THE RIVER SLEA
◆❀◆

The gaunt ruins of Haverholme Priory are like a setting from a film. It was the very place where Thomas à Beckett hid for a couple of days from the wrath of the King after the Council of Northampton and it was also used by Charles Dickens as Cherney Wold in his book 'Bleak House'. The walk by the canalised River Slea is a pleasant, easy stroll with some surprising sculpture to be discovered en route.

The River Slea.

There are seven locks along the 13-mile length of the Navigation from Sleaford through Anwick and South Kyme to the River Witham at Chapel Hill. Five of these locks are within the 4 miles between Sleaford and Anwick. Most of the towpath along the Navigation is a public right of way and Lincolnshire County Council once agreed to it being designated as a medium distance footpath as part of the Two Canals Way linking the Trent to the Witham via the Grantham Canal and the Sleaford Navigation. It is said that the Romans made a road from Sleaford to Horncastle which ran straight through Ewerby and over the

Roman Car Dyke to North Kyme where there was a Roman settlement. More important than this road however was the River Slea, which divided into two arms, passing close to the west of Evedon, then turning east past the north of Ewerby and combining again into one stream at Cobblers Lock. These two arms of the River Slea enclosed a large island or 'holme' and were an important route for water-borne traffic down the ages. Before 1066 these lands belonged to Leofric, Earl of Mercia and were left in the hands of his famous widow, Lady Godiva. After the Conquest, King William distributed the spoils of war to his Norman companions, and Bishop Remigus who built Lincoln cathedral and Gilbert de Gaunt, Lord of Kyme, received most of this land. Gilbert's daughter, Maud married Ralph FitzOoth. Their son William had a son Robert FitzOoth, better known in history and legend as Robin Hood!

At the 16th century Dissolution of the Monasteries, the great Gilbertine Haverholme Priory for the training and educating of nuns and canons was given to Edward Lord Clinton. The Gothic house first built on the site of the old Priory was poorly constructed but later much improved by being encased in Ancaster stone in Tudor style. During this work lidless coffins of nuns of old were unearthed. The great mansion of 132 rooms was demolished in 1927 and only the stables, a lodge house and a ruined section still remain. The long avenue had an odd reputation with a tradition that it was haunted by a Gilbertine canoness being seen by a particular tree by the bridge over Ruskington Beck. Various families held the land surrounding Haverholme Priory and in 1763 it was sold to Sir William Gordon. Sir Jennison Gordon followed and he was the Chairman of the first public meeting called to consider canalising the River Slea. Sir Jennison was a great gardener and he intended to leave the Haverholme Estate to one of his cousins. When the chosen cousin chanced to admire a weed (silverweed) Sir Jennison was so affronted that he returned to the Priory and immediately altered his will, leaving the Priory and 3,700 acres to another cousin, George William Finch-Hatton, who later became the 10th Earl of Winchilsea. The 12th Earl of Winchilsea and Nottingham resided in the rebuilt Haverholme Priory and he owned most of Ewerby village. His daughter, Lady Muriel Finch-Hatton, after hospital-work in the 1914-18 war, devoted her life to helping the sick and poor of Russia and the Baltic states and was made a C.B.E. in 1938. The broach spire of St Andrew's church has been said to be the most beautiful in England. There are some interesting monuments in the church.

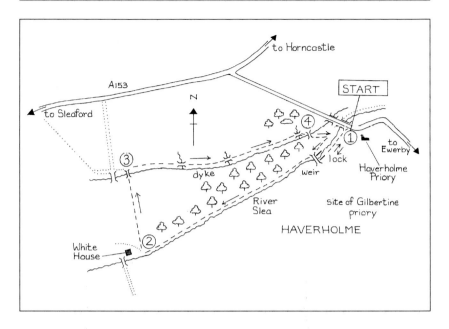

The Finch Hatton Arms just 1½ miles down the Ewerby road, is a delightful free house to be recommended for its decor, well-kept beer and standard of food. Engraved on a glass door is a saying of Oscar Wilde's: 'I have the simplest tastes: I am always satisfied with the best.' Meals are served from 12 noon until 2 pm and from 6.30 pm until 10 pm. Telephone: 01529 460363.

- **HOW TO GET THERE:** On the A153 driving towards Horncastle from the Sleaford direction, turn right off the main road just over 1 mile beyond the sharp Ruskington bend. Proceeding towards Sleaford, turn left off the main road 1 mile beyond Anwick village.
- **PARKING:** There is a small car park signposted on the right immediately after Haverholme Bridge.
- **LENGTH OF THE WALK:** 1¾ miles. Map: OS Landranger 130 Grantham and surrounding area (GR 102499).

THE WALK

1 From the car park proceed through the iron kissing gate (without the gate) and turn left to walk down a clear edge-boarded path with the River Slea on your right. Pause to look at the attractive wooden sculpture of a fox and pheasant at the side of the path and the gaunt ruin of a once great house across the field over on the left. On reaching the canal lock note the remains of the pump built to supply water from the river first to the Priory and later to Ewerby. Cross the bridge above the foaming weir and then the planked walkway over the spillway to turn left along the rather overgrown old towpath with ancient, neglected woodland on the right. Continue for about 1,000 yards.

2 On reaching the stile, a handgate across the towpath and a waymark turn right away from the river with the new garden fence on the immediate left. Leave this path after 50 yards to turn right (yellow waymark) into the wood edge. The red waymark for continuing straight on indicates a 'Road used as a Public Path' but it would be rather difficult to get a horse and cart down the path. Follow the wood edge until the wooded section of the path ends and walk straight forward across the field to the obvious newly-erected wooden bridge over a wide dyke. Cross the bridge.

3 Turn right with the dyke on your immediate right and continue forward over three new bridges. After the third bridge, this one of sloping railway sleepers, turn right.

4 Almost immediately cross another bridge this time over the main dyke and turn diagonally left across the pasture field, walking just to the left of the small copse of trees to a stile in the fence and a metal signpost. Climb the stile and turn right along an attractive path back to the lock and weir. Cross the bridge once again to turn left back to the car park.

PLACES OF INTEREST NEARBY

Cogglesford Water Mill at Sleaford is open Easter to October daily, 10 am until 4 pm. Admission free (donations welcome). The Woodland Trust has two sites nearby – *Sleaford Wood* (GR 073469) covers some 26 acres, and *High Wood* at North Rauceby (GR 010462) about 31 acres.

WALK 15

WOOLSTHORPE BY BELVOIR

There are some splendid views to be enjoyed on this walk, with the story-book castle at Belvoir visible for much of the time. The outward route is a stroll along the Grantham Canal, returning by the little River Devon.

The Grantham Canal.

Beware, for there are two Woolsthorpes less than ten miles apart. Woolsthorpe by Belvoir is in Lincolnshire but only just. The Leicestershire border is yards away to the west and the Nottinghamshire border is about 4 miles down the canal. This is a pleasant place with open fields, woods and rolling hills that belie the tale that Lincolnshire is entirely flat. Originally an estate village there are now some private houses. It remains a hunting area though and the Belvoir Hunt hounds are kept nearby. Belvoir Castle is the seat of the Duke of Rutland. During the Civil War it withstood a siege for four months before surrendering. It was then demolished in 1649. Rebuilding began shortly afterwards with major additions in the 18th and 19th centuries. Cromwell's soldiers stationing their horses in the church at Woolsthorpe set the bedding straw alight on their departure and as a result of the fire getting out of control the church was burnt down. The village now has another church. Just off the walk route, Brewers Grave is reputedly the burial place of one of the brewers from Belvoir Castle who drowned in his own vat of ale! The Grantham Canal, begun in 1793, is nearby. It is 33 miles in length and rises 129 feet to Grantham by a series of 18 locks that admitted barges 75 foot long and 14 foot wide. As in so many cases it was the arrival of the railway, also from Nottingham, in July 1850 which heralded the decline of the canal. At least it survived into the 20th century but by 1929 trade had almost ceased and it was legally 'abandoned' in 1936. However, the Grantham Canal Restoration Society has been working towards the day when the waterway can be opened for traffic once more – this time for pleasure.

The Chequers Inn displays a chess or chequer board to suggest the passing away of an odd hour by a game of 'draughts'. Apparently there are 270 hotels, taverns or inns in England bearing this sign. Nestling at the base of a steeply wooded slope and with a large cricket pitch behind this is a pleasant country inn now offering accommodation and food. It is a free house with a good range of real ale, including Brewster's. A Brewster is an old English word for a female brewer. Sara Barton, born in the Vale of Belvoir, has a Masters Degree in Brewing and has started Brewster's Brewing Company locally producing a range of premium cask ales made from 100% natural ingredients. There is Winter Strong Ale, Spring Golden Ale and Summer Wheat Beer. Meals are served from 12 noon until 2 pm and evening meals from 7 pm until 9 pm.

Telephone: 01476 870701.

- **HOW TO GET THERE:** From the A607 Grantham to Melton Mowbray road, turn off at Denton crossroads signposted Woolsthorpe by Belvoir. From the A52(T) Grantham to Nottingham road, turn off by Sedgebrook.
- **PARKING:** In the car park of the Chequers Inn, Woolsthorpe by Belvoir (with the kind permission of the landlord). If necessary additional parking is available at the edge of the cricket field behind the inn.
- **LENGTH OF THE WALK:** 4½ miles. Map: OS Landranger 130 Grantham and surrounding area (GR 838341).

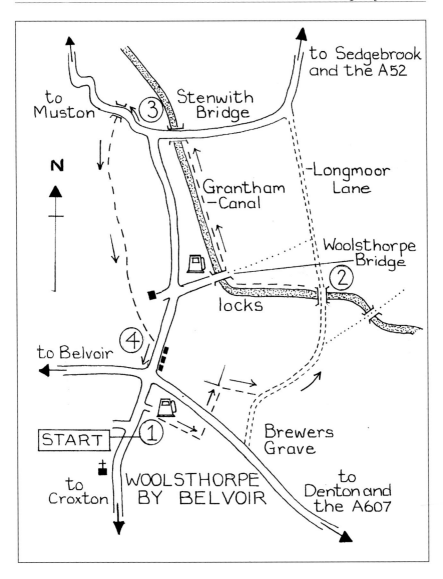

THE WALK

1 From the Chequers Inn car park walk up the right-hand side of the cricket field until you reach the small white hut with cricket score panels. Directly behind this hut you will discover a home-made stile. Cross the stile and then walk forward to the wood. Continue upwards with Fanny's Wood on your immediate left. There is a wonderful view

The pub at the start of the walk.

from here across the Vale and Belvoir Castle stands out like a child's picture-book castle. On coming to a stile, signpost and waymark for the Jubilee Way, turn left over the stile and take the right-hand stoned track through the woodland to the road. Walk straight across the road and over the grass field to the hedge. At the corner of this hedge turn diagonally right on a marked track to the right-hand field corner, where there are signposts. Turn left along the overgrown Longmoor Lane (the Viking Way) with a very attractive view of wooded, rolling hills leading down into the valley. The canal and the incredible Harlaxton Manor can be seen over on the right. (See Places of Interest Nearby at the end of the walk.)

2 On reaching the canal cross the bridge and turn left along the canal towpath. Continue to the locks at Woolsthorpe Bridge. The Rutland Arms (locally called 'The Mucky Duck' and a close inspection of the weather vane will reveal why) is just across the canal. Continue along the wide stretch of grass with an abandoned mineral railway on the right. Bear right away from the canal to the road. The oak ladder stile is in memory of Hedley Lewis, the first Council Chairman of the amalgamated County of Lincolnshire (Holland, Lindsey and Kesteven) and my predecessor as Area President of the Ramblers' Association,

Lincolnshire. He was instrumental in devising and bringing to fruition the idea of a long distance recreational path across Lincolnshire that eventually became The Viking Way. Turn left down the lane to Stenwith Bridge.

3 Continue down the lane, ignoring the lane on the left leading back to Woolsthorpe. On reaching the next little bridge after about 300 yards turn left on a signposted footpath by a stile with the little River Devon (pronounced Deevon) on your left. Cross the little footbridge and stile over a newly cleared dyke and continue forward with the river on your left for about 800 yards until you meet an old stone bridge. Turn left over the bridge and follow the path round to the right with the river now on your right. At a stile in the cross-hedge see the friendly notice from the farmer at Grange Farm over on your left. It reads: 'Hope you are enjoying your walk on this land' and explains about pollarding the riverside willows. Walk diagonally left across the arable field on a clearly marked public footpath to the road.

4 Climb the roadside embankment and turn right with the Hunt Cottages across the road on the left. Continue along the road back into the village. Go straight across the crossroads and turn left into the Chequers Inn car park.

PLACES OF INTEREST NEARBY
From the walk at Longmoor Lane *Harlaxton Manor* may be seen 3 miles away across the valley. It is now used by the University of Evansville but the gardens are open daily for visitors from April until October between 11 am and 5 pm, except on Monday. It is well worth a visit. Telephone: 01476 564541.

Belvoir Castle is open from 31st March until 1st October, Tuesday to Thursday and Saturday from 11 am until 3 pm. Admission charge. Telephone: 01476 870262.

FOSDYKE BRIDGE AND THE SALT MARSHES

꙳

Rich reclaimed agricultural land, a nature reserve and easy walking on the top of sea banks, with extensive views over Kirton salt marsh, enhance this exhilarating walk where the River Welland meets the Wash. There is excellent coastal bird watching, especially during the winter months.

The Ship Inn, Fosdyke Bridge.

Most of the Lincolnshire waterways were at one time Navigations, that is, a promoting company took over and controlled existing rivers and made them navigable for trade. The earliest in the county and one of the earliest in the country at large to be established by Act of Parliament was on the River Welland, downstream at Stamford in 1570. A constant struggle was needed to maintain them, for drainage schemes and other changes in land use meant that the rivers often altered or silted up their courses. Prisoners of war have often been used as cheap labour. Dutch prisoners of war taken in battle more than 300 years ago worked on the original drainage of the Fens, and after the Battle of Dunbar in 1650 when the entire Scottish army was overthrown by Cromwell's Commonwealth soldiers, 10,000 prisoners were put to work on various projects, the majority digging out rivers and drains. Descendants of the Dutch and Scottish prisoners of war remain in the Fen today. During the Second World War German and Italian prisoners of war were set to help on the land and to repair breaches on river banks. History repeated itself and former POWs from 1939 to 1946 may still be found in the district today. As you walk you cannot help but be aware of the efforts made to reclaim the land of the Fen. Less peacefully, the nearby bombing range at RAF Holbeach is in full use throughout the year, often with NATO planes, and there are some spectacular fly-pasts of aircraft both British and foreign. They are less likely to be flying at weekends.

The Ship Inn is a cosy roadside pub by the busy A17. It belongs to our own Lincolnshire Brewery serving Bateman's Good Honest Ales and provides popular, freshly prepared and excellent value for money food. Indeed a notice outside states 'Great Food'.

Telephone: 01205 260628.

- **HOW TO GET THERE:** Driving southwards on the A17(T) 20 miles south of Sleaford, cross the Fosdyke Bridge, pass the Bridge Inn and after 500 yards turn left up Middle Marsh Road. Driving northwards towards Sleaford turn right off the main road up Middle Marsh Road before crossing the bridge. After 1¾ miles turn left at the road junction for 350 yards to the nature reserve on your left.
- **PARKING:** By the nature reserve, entrance off Middle Marsh Road.
- **LENGTH OF THE WALK:** 3 miles. Map: OS Landranger 131 Boston and Spalding area (GR 344336).

THE WALK

1 From the parking space by the nature reserve enter the reserve along the old sea bank parallel to Middle Marsh Farm with a deep dyke on your right. At the end of the reserve turn right towards the River Welland and right again on the river bank until you reach the jetty.

2 A motorable track leads back to where you parked on the right but walk straight on along the top of the new sea bank with the River Welland on the left and an enormous drop on your right. There are

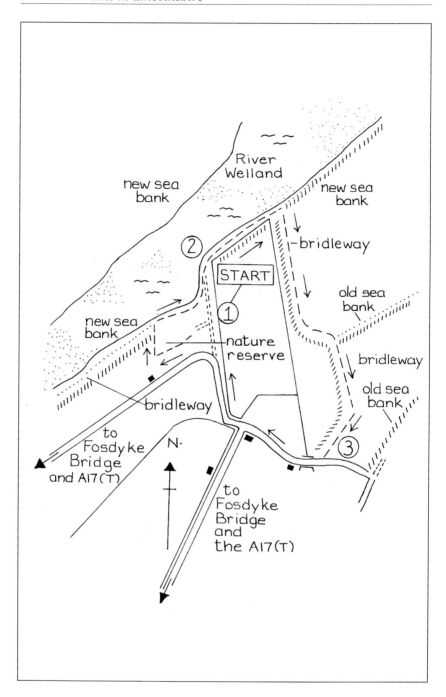

The River Welland embankment near Fosdyke Bridge.

incredible names for the sand banks at the river's outfall into the Wash – Puff, Blue Back, Mare Tail, Inner Gat and Herring Hill. Continue forward for about 550 yards. Leave the river bank to turn right on a signposted bridleway along another old sea bank and continue along the top of this bank for almost 1 mile until you reach the lane.

3 Turn right along the road and continue straight forward ignoring the lane on the left after 550 yards. The building on the corner was once a public house but is now a private dwelling. Walk on the road or on the top of the bank past Middle Marsh Road back to your starting place.

PLACES OF INTEREST NEARBY
Fydell House is undoubtedly the grandest house in Boston. It is situated adjacent to the Guildhall in South Square and is open to visitors in University term times from Monday to Thursday from 10 am until 12.30 pm and 1.30 pm until 4 pm from Monday to Thursday and closing earlier at 3.30 pm on Fridays. The telephone number is 01205 351520. Also in Boston, *Hussey Tower*, built about 1450 can be seen from Skirbeck Lane. It is open from dawn to dusk. Telephone: 01529 461499.

HAUNTED THURLBY

A beautiful and ancient church with some Anglo-Saxon work, a splendid section of the Roman Car Dyke, a haunted wood, the well-kept Lawrance Park, a pleasant pub and some well-marked public footpaths over arable fields all make this a memorable walk.

The Car Dyke, near Thurlby.

There are more than 250 place names in Lincolnshire ending in the Danish 'by' (meaning village or farmstead). The routes followed by those land-hungry settlers seem to have been along the rivers and especially the Roman roads, for many Danish place-names lie within easy reach of such a road. In places they may have taken over an Anglian settlement (sometimes renaming it) and then established hamlets in outlying parts of the lands belonging to the original settlement. At Thurlby there are Northorpe, Southorpe and Obthorpe – 'thorpe' meaning an outlying farmstead. It has been put forward that the original Anglo-Saxon name for the village was changed by the Danes in the early 8th or 9th centuries to Turulf's village, modified later as Thurlby. The parish church dedication to St Firmin, who was the Bishop of Amiens in France and martyred by the Emperor Diocletian, is almost unique in this country, sharing it with just one other church in England – that of North Crawley, Newport Pagnell, Bucks. It may be that there was a Romano-British church on this site before AD 400 but the oldest parts of the present building have been dated about AD 925. The old vicarage, long since demolished, was supposed to be haunted but it has been said that the story was invented simply to discourage visitors after dark! In Elsea Wood, on your route, the pool is supposed to be haunted. Nanny Rutt was a servant girl at one of the houses in the village. She disappeared after having a dream about being murdered by her boy friend at the well and was never seen again.

The Horseshoe Inn situated by Thurlby crossroads is a pleasant, Mansfield house that has had an extensive refurbishment and is now under new management. Traditional bar meals are available.

Telephone: 01778 421576.

- **HOW TO GET THERE:** Thurlby is 2 miles south of Bourne on the A15 Sleaford to Peterborough road.
- **PARKING:** At the crossroads in Thurlby village, turn off the main road for the car park by St Firmin's church. Alternatively use the Horseshoe Inn car park (by kind permission of the landlord).
- **LENGTH OF THE WALK:** 3½ miles. Map: OS Landranger 130 Grantham and surrounding area (GR 105167).

THE WALK

1 From the church car park walk straight forward across the lane that leads down to Thurlby Fen and along a narrow, signposted tarmac track leading after a few yards to a decrepit bridge. Climb the stile and turn right with the Car Dyke on your immediate right. Go through the wooden fieldgate to cross the track leading to the Manor School and follow the signposted footpath to the new stout bridge with handrails. Cross the bridge and turn left with the Dyke now on your left. After 800 yards cross Fen Lane and continue forward for another 800 yards to the next bridge.

2 Turn left down the short track to the Bourne road. Cross the road with care and enter Elsea Wood on a signposted, wandering pathway. Continue straight forward on a meandering track with occasional waymarks on trees. You go from one wood to another without any

79

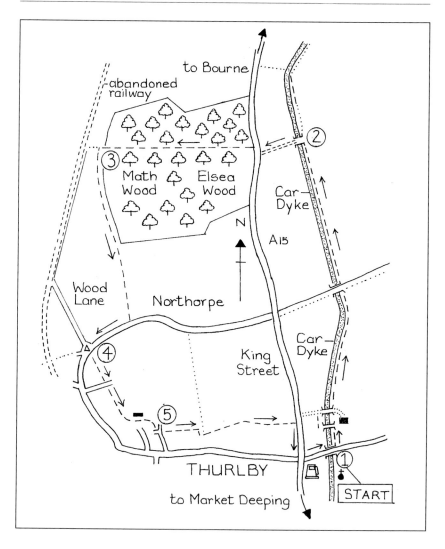

distinguishing features except that Math Wood may be slightly more muddy.

3 At the wood edge you will discover a footbridge. Continue forward into the open field for only a few yards and then turn left (waymark) with the wood edge now on your left. Continue forward on a clear path after the end of the wood. When you reach the end of the field turn right for a few yards only before turning left over a ditchboard. At the end of the hedge continue straight forward to a wooden gate (waymark) leading you through the garden of a house to the lane. There is a public footpath signpost half hidden in the bush on the right. Turn right along Northorpe village street for about 300 yards.

4 On reaching the grass triangle and the beginning of Wood Lane turn left on a signposted path to a kissing gate and keep along the field edge with garden boundaries upon your immediate right. Continue straight across the estate road and the path leads you down into the extensive recreation area known as Lawrance Park. A few years ago two ladies, members of the Lawrance family, who owned land in the village gave land to be used as a playing field. This has now been developed into a park and as well as a playing field there is a modern village hall and a new primary school. A cup was also given by the two ladies to be presented annually to the person or group of persons who had done outstanding voluntary work for the benefit of the village. Walk forward with the school buildings and modern village hall on your left to turn left after the school and continue straight forward over the recreational field.

5 Keep to the right-hand edge of the field around the corner until you reach a footpath entry into the small estate. There is an obvious space in the wooden perimeter fence here. The short path leads you into a cul-de-sac. Turn left at Park View and then go straight across the estate road on a signposted public footpath between houses. Turn right at the field edge and at the end of the ditch continue straight forward towards the main road, here the Roman King Street. Turn right to the crossroads and the Horseshoe Inn. If your starting place was the church car park it is 150 yards up the lane from the crossroads.

PLACES OF INTEREST NEARBY
At the very end of the lane (about 1½ miles) after turning right from the church car park is *Thurlby Slipe*. The Lincolnshire Trust has acquired the water meadows on the banks of the River Glen and visitors are welcome. *Bourne Wood*, part of the primeval forest of Brunswald, is also open for visitors. There are 700 acres with Corsican pine but plenty of native trees such as oak, ash, beech and the small-leaved lime. There is a car park, and easy rides and paths with some surprising sculptures en route.

WALK 18

SPALDING AND THE RIVER WELLAND

Driving across the wide, open panorama of the Fen, Spalding is a remarkably pleasant discovery. The town has a real character of its own, enhanced by the River Welland flowing through and the streets and attractive walkways on both sides of the river. This is a wonderful walk of contrasts, alongside waterways for the whole of the route. You will find walking some stretches of the Coronation Channel is quite remote and even pleasantly lonely, although less than a mile from the High Street.

The River Welland.

Spalding, the most important town of the Lincolnshire Fens which spread for 10 miles or more of unbroken flatness in every direction, is the centre of the most fertile land in England. Flowers blossom under a vast expanse of glass for horticulture has become a great industry here. Millions of blooms go by rail and road to all parts of the country.

Sugar beet and potatoes and, of course, bulbs dominate the agriculture of the district and miles of plastic sheets on the fields look like a strange inland sea. It is an ancient town with the tree-lined roads on either side of the River Welland forming an attractive feature, enhanced today by the provision of cycle/walkways. By the High Bridge, not far from the market place and at the corner of Church Gate and Church Street, stands the old White Horse Inn built in the early 17th century, white-walled, thatched, picturesque and inviting. The church of St Mary and St Nicholas, set well back in a churchyard, was built as a parish church in 1284. There are some lovely old trees, lime, sycamore and ash. The town developed out of a Benedictine priory founded in 1087. This priory became one of the richest religious houses in England. The wealth of the town depended upon the river, the main trade route for the import of coal, timber and foodstuffs and the export of agricultural produce.

Ayscoughfee Hall and its gardens, where the walk starts, are a treasure, and should not be missed. It is a grand old mansion of brick and stone open to visitors as a museum and information centre with an attractive cafe in the grounds. The war memorial at the end of a long formal garden pool is beautifully sited.

The White Horse Inn near the Hall is a rare Lincolnshire thatched pub that once featured in the 'Old Inns' series of Wills' cigarette cards in the late 1930s. It is an unspoilt and friendly pub built out of the materials of the former Benedictine Priory and certainly one of the oldest buildings in town. The building was originally built as a residence and shop in 1553 and known, at that time, as Berguery House.

There were once four other rival inns in the vicinity and the wily publican of Ye Olde White Horse once inscribed the following under his sign:

'My White Horse shall bite the Bear
And make the Angel fly
Shall turn the Ship her bottom up
And drink the Three Cups dry.'

The White Horse of today remains an historic inn with a character all of its own. It is a Samuel Smith's (Tadcaster) house serving a range of their well-kept, hand-pumped real ales plus guest beers. Good value food is provided daily and all visitors will find a pleasant atmosphere and a warm welcome. Telephone: 01775 766740.

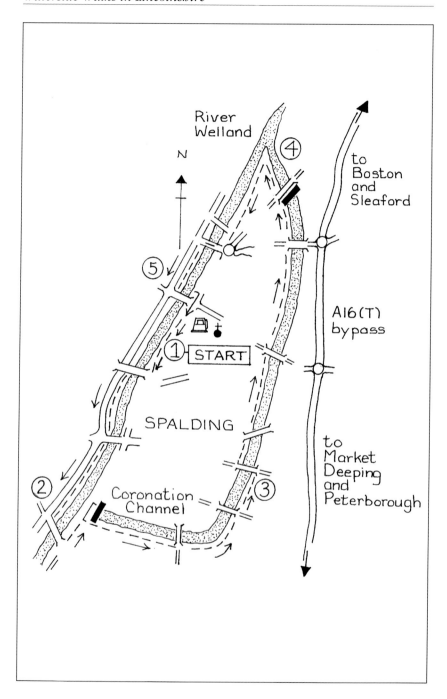

War memorial and pool in Ayscoughfee Gardens.

- **HOW TO GET THERE:** Take the A16(T) Boston to Stamford road. Turn off the new bypass into Spalding at the Holbeach Road roundabout. Continue into town with the River Welland on the right down High Street and Churchgate to find parking.
- **PARKING:** Various parking places with some roadside parking by Ayscoughfee Hall at the side of the river, where the walk starts. There is a large free car park at Holland Road on the left of High Street.
- **LENGTH OF THE WALK:** 4½ miles. Map: OS Landranger 131 Boston and Spalding area (GR 250224).

THE WALK

1 From Ayscoughfee Hall main entrance cross the road to turn left for about 200 yards on the footway alongside the river on your right. Cross over the Victoria footbridge and turn left along the riverside path for about 1,000 yards until you reach the old railway bridge with the footway on the far side.

2 Cross the river once again and turn left for a few yards until you reach the massive lock gates of the Coronation Channel built in 1953 to relieve the town of flooding. Turn right along the bank on the clearly marked footpath with the water on your left. Continue on the same bank across Spalding Drove Bridge, Childers South Drove Bridge and Childers North Drove Bridge.

3 There is a footpath on both sides but at Childers North Drove Bridge (the third) cross over the bridge to walk along the other bank simply to distance yourself from the bypass traffic noise. You pass a disused railway bridge on your right. Continue along this Coronation Channel path for another three bridges, Low Road, Holbeach Road and Marsh Road in that order, until you meet another set of massive lock gates at Marsh Road. Go straight across the road to follow a signposted footpath for about 100 yards until you reach the junction with the River Welland.

4 Turn left here with the River Welland on your immediate right. Ignore the first river crossing and walk on to the roundabout. Turn right over the river and left to walk down the riverside footway along Albion Street and then Double Street.

5 On reaching High Bridge cross the river once again and turn right with the splendid White Horse Inn on your left. Continue along Churchgate to your starting place at Ayscoughfee Hall main entrance.

PLACES OF INTEREST NEARBY

There is much to see in and around Spalding. *Ayscoughfee Hall* is a medieval hall with eight museum galleries and gardens. Open all the year except winter weekends from 10 am until 5 pm, admission free. Telephone: 01775 725468. The *Gordon Boswell Romany Museum* at Clay Lake, Spalding is open March to October every day from 10 am until 5.30 pm. Admission charge.

Spalding Bulb Museum and Horticultural Exhibition at Pinchbeck is open daily April to October from 10 am until 4 pm, admission free. Telephone: 01775 680490. Also at Pinchbeck is the *Engine and Land Drainage Museum*, with a fine working beam engine of the kind used to drain the Fens. Admission free. Open daily April to October, 10 am until 4 pm. Telephone: 01775 725468.

WEST DEEPING AND THE RIVER WELLAND

Cross the county boundary on this walk along the banks of both little-known branches of the upper River Welland. The route begins in the delightful village of West Deeping, inhabited long before the Romans came, takes in a section of the ancient King Street and two magnificent old water mills.

The River Welland between West Deeping and Market Deeping.

'The Deepings' is an evocative name but the truth is that the Welland used to flood every year and Deeping or Deeping Meadows was the origin of the name. It has now become a collective name for the group of five villages built along the Welland. West Deeping was old when Market Deeping was still a swamp. As everywhere the Romans converted earlier prehistoric tracks into straight metalled roads – King Street as constructed by the Romans only upgraded a former prehistoric trackway whose origins are lost in the mists of time. Many prehistoric relics have been uncovered in the gravel workings of the Deepings and often their value has not been recognised. A large stone used by one family as a door-stop was in fact the tooth of a mammoth. Relics of an ancient forest that once covered the land were collected for fences and one farmer made a complete fence around his farmyard entirely of fossilized timber. Archaeologists have made some exciting finds, including the bones of an Ice-Age elephant near Deeping St James. The remains of a Bronze Age farming community was unearthed nearby. The elephant was a 120,000 year old straight-tusked elephant, with one tusk being twelve feet long. It is now being reassembled in Peterborough museum.

Set back from the modern high road, West Deeping is the smallest of the Deepings and surely the most attractive. Its houses line almost ½ mile of the Roman King Street and the lovely view of the church and watermill across the meadow from the one-arched bridge deserves to be better known. One of the shields in the church is probably that of the Black Prince, who married Joan, the Fair Maid of Kent. She was heiress of the Wakes whose great possessions included all of the Deepings. The manor house, a Grade II listed building, was built in 1643 with a surrounding moat. It was once owned by Margaret Beaufort, mother of Henry VII.

Early pub landlords were often retired stewards of the nobility. They had a tendency to reproduce the armorial bearings of their former employer as signs for the new hostelries, which soon became known locally by the most prominent feature displayed on the Coat of Arms. Many an heraldic lion was promptly dubbed the Red Lion by its unlettered patrons as a result. A Red Lion inn sign is fairly common in Lincolnshire for it was the badge of John of Gaunt, Duke of Lancaster, whose son, Henry IV, was born at Bolingbroke Castle, near Spilsby. The Red Lion at West Deeping is an attractive, friendly old stone-built pub with low beamed ceilings and an open fire. It is a free house serving a range of well-kept, hand-pumped beers and draught cider. There is an interesting and unusual menu and meals are served from 12 noon until 2.30 pm and from 6 pm until 9.30 pm.

Telephone: 01778 347190.

- **HOW TO GET THERE:** On the A15 Bourne to Peterborough road, turn off towards Stamford from the Market Deeping northern roundabout on the new bypass. Take the A16(T) Stamford road for 1½ miles and then the first road left into West Deeping.

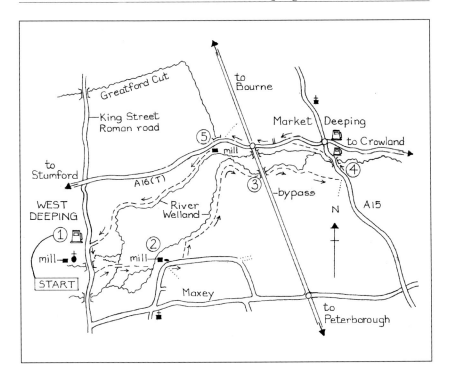

- **PARKING:** In the large car park of the Red Lion Inn, King Street, West Deeping (by kind permission of the landlord).
- **LENGTH OF THE WALK:** 4½ miles. Map: OS Landranger 142 Peterborough and surrounding area (GR 110088).

THE WALK

1 From the Red Lion car park turn right down King Street until you reach the first humped back old road bridge. However, the church and watermill on the right are certainly worth a brief detour. A few yards beyond the road bridge turn left on a signposted public footpath with a branch of the Welland on your left. Fishing has always been a popular activity on the Welland with eel catching carried out at the start of the century. Roach, chubb and pike live on the river today. Cross the stout footbridge and walk up the field edge to a stile. There is a confusion of waterways hereabouts and you now have water for the mill race on your right as well as the Welland on the left. Cross the weir and the attractive lawn of Maxey Mill and go over the stile at the side of the entrance onto the lane.

2 Turn left at the lane for about 100 yards and left again off the lane onto a signposted, bridged, waymarked footpath with a small dyke and intermittent coppice on the left, until you reach the main stream. Continue along this attractive bank for about a mile until you reach another weir with water on the right in addition to the main stream on the left. Do not cross the weir bridge (there is a notice saying 'Private') but turn right alongside the new waterway and follow it around the bend to the bypass.

3 Go under the bypass with the road bridge above and the stream on your immediate left. Building the Deepings bypass revealed further archaeological discoveries including extensive Bronze Age and Roman remains and a burial ground complete with skeletons. The road was raised so that the burial ground would remain undamaged. No one will be able to get at the remains or excavate them and they should remain there undisturbed for generations. The area is on your right as you walk below the bypass. Continue on the clear path by the waterside through the small grove of trees. At the end of the tree belt bear diagonally right across the field, aiming initially towards a small group of three or four isolated trees and then on to the stile and signpost by the main road.

The river seen from the grounds of the Old Coach House pub.

4 Turn left towards the bridge and after crossing turn left again with the river now on your left. The Old Coach House across the bridge is a pleasant place for a break. Your path leads behind the houses and continues along to the end where it meets the main Stamford Road. Turn left up to the bypass and cross with care. Continue straight forward until you meet the superb Molecy House and Mill on the left.

5 At the end of the house grounds turn left on a signposted footpath, at first up a pleasant wide green track that soon descends into an ordinary footpath width. The path follows a fence and then on your left yet another branch of the River Welland. The path becomes a farm accommodation track that leads you into the abandoned farm buildings with a wide centre turning space. Your path leads out at the top left-hand side of this area and down a little lane to King Street, and the Red Lion a few yards away on the right.

PLACES OF INTEREST NEARBY

At *Crowland Abbey*, Church Lane, Crowland, you will find the awe-inspiring ruins of a great Fenland Abbey, now a parish church. The profile of the great west tower dominates the landscape. Telephone: 01733 210499. The *Peakirk Waterfowl Gardens*, near Peterborough has 20 acres of gardens and lakes. Admission charge. Open daily 9.30 am until 5.30 pm (1 hour before dusk in winter). Telephone: 01733 252271. *Flag Fen*, Fourth Drove, Fengate, Peterborough, is one of Europe's most important prehistoric excavation sites. Telephone: 01733 313414. Admission charge. Open all the year.

WINGLAND AND
THE PETER SCOTT WAY

This unusual and beautiful linear walk is very remote, following the Peter Scott Way to skirt the estuary between the Nene outfall and the River Great Ouse by wild and impressive salt marshes and tidal flats which are very important to wild life.

The sea bank bridleway by the River Nene.

An unlikely name, Wingland, yet there it is on a road sign! Perhaps it was named originally on account of the number and variety of birds that may be seen in the area during breeding and migration. The whole of this Wash Estuary has been designated a Site of Special Scientific Interest. It is also a Ramsar Site, that is, a wetland of international importance. The River Nene Channel on your left during your seaward walk has the incredible name of Tycho Wing's Channel. If arrangements can be made to be met at Ongar Hill it is possible to take a 7-mile linear walk along the Peter Scott Way. Details of how to get to

Ongar Hill are given at the end of the walk. However, most walkers may simply walk out to the point or as far as you wish along the 1974 sea bank and return by the same route. Unfortunately, the parallel, very attractive 1953 tree-clad bank is not a public right of way. The Way is a bridleway in Lincolnshire but becomes a footpath at the Norfolk border. One cannot get lost – it is along the top of the outermost sea bank for much of the route and below the bank on a good track at the Ongar Hill end.

Peter Scott, naturalist, painter and conservationist, the son of the explorer Captain Scott of the Antarctic, lived in the East Bank Lighthouse at Sutton Bridge for six years in the 1930s at a rent of £5 a year. The lighthouse had four storeys with one room on each floor and during his stay he added a bunk room, a garage, a studio and an entrance porch. A local poacher, Mr Mackenzie Thorpe, known as 'Kenzie, the Wild Goose Man', came to tend the wildfowl that Scott had begun to collect and tame. At that time spring tides surrounded the lighthouse on three sides. A best-selling book, *The Snow Goose* by Peter Gallico was written about one of Peter Scott's birds here at East Bank Lighthouse. A plaque on the old lighthouse records his stay on this remote part of the Lincolnshire coast. Sir Peter Scott opened the Peter Scott Walk in April 1989 just before he died. It is a 10-mile linear route from East Bank Lighthouse to West Lynn in Norfolk, where a small passenger ferry across the River Great Ouse takes people to King's Lynn throughout the year.

The rambling Bridge Hotel down by the riverside stands well back now that the approach road to the bridge has been realigned and the old section of the road has become a useful parking place. In the hotel bar there is an expanse of carpet, comfortable seating and a warm atmosphere. Tetley's Bitter, Ansell's Mild, Carlsberg Export, Carlsberg Lager, Scrumpy Jack Cider and draught Guinness are on offer. Normal bar meals are served from 11.30 am until 2 pm. A separate dining room and a large function room cater for more formal occasions. Telephone: 01406 350222.

- **HOW TO GET THERE:** Proceeding southwards on the A17(T) road towards King's Lynn, turn left onto a minor road signed Wingland, immediately after crossing the Cross Keys Bridge over the River Nene. Driving northwards towards Boston on the A17(T) road, turn right immediately before the bridge.

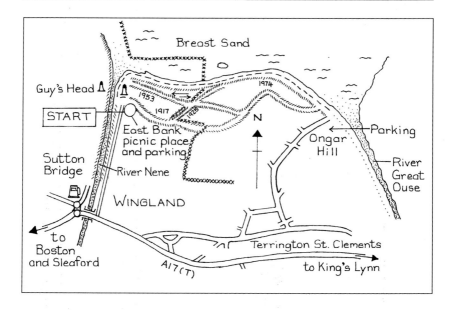

- **PARKING:** East Bank Picnic Place and Car Park is situated almost at the end of this 2¾ mile road just before the lighthouse. Turn right off the metalled road down the steep entry into the car park, with a notice requesting visitors not to park on the grass.
- **LENGTH OF THE WALK:** Any length up to 7 miles. Map: OS Landranger 131 Boston and Spalding area (GR 493255).

THE WALK

From the car park go through the kissing gate and up the small embankment to walk towards the lighthouse. Proceed through the kissing gate on the left. Climb the embankment steps by the lighthouse and continue along the top of the sea wall towards the Wash. Turn right on reaching the point and follow the Peter Scott Way for as far as you wish before retracing your steps.

After leaving the main road the last farm you come to is Lighthouse Farm and across the river, some way inland today, is King John's Farm. This marks the place where King John is supposed to have lost the crown jewels and his wardrobe when, in October 1216, the whole baggage train was swept away by the incoming tide or swallowed up in the treacherous quicksands. Not a man survived to tell the tale. King John, who travelled a longer but safer route, died two days later.

TO GET TO ONGAR HILL: Driving towards King's Lynn, 1½ miles

Sutton Bridge over the Nene.

beyond Terrington St Clements at Grid Ref 569203, turn left signed Terrington Marsh. Go round the left-hand bend and almost immediately turn right, still following signs to Terrington Marsh. At the telephone and letter box fork right, signed Ongar Hill. Follow the road to the end, where there is parking space just over the embankment.

PLACES OF INTEREST NEARBY
The Bridge Hotel has played its part in the history of *Sutton Bridge* as it has been associated with the RAF since 1926 when a summer camp for airmen was opened. The RAF camp soon became an Operational Training Unit because the flat and sparsely populated land was suitable for bombing and firing practice. Many Battle of Britain pilots trained at Sutton Bridge. In the village church the altar in the north aisle was dedicated to airmen who were killed during their stay at the station and an oak tablet records all their names. Pilot training ceased in 1946.

The *Butterfly and Falconry Park* at Long Sutton is open daily, 28th March to 1st November, 10 am to 6 pm. Admission charge. Telephone: 01406 383833. The *African Violet Centre*, Terrington St Clements, is open daily 10 am to 5 pm (tea room – Easter until October). Admission free. Telephone: 01553 828374.